DOUBLE YOUR SALARY, BONK YOUR BOSS, GO HOME EARLY

GUY BROWNING

DOUBLE YOUR SALARY,

BONK YOUR BOSS,

GO HOME EARLY

GUY BROWNING

Virgin

Illustrations by Mathew Woodall.

This work is dedicated to Judith Condor because it's easier than getting her dedicated to work.

First published in 1997 by
Virgin Books
an imprint of Virgin Publishing Ltd
332 Ladbroke Grove
London W10 5AH

A catalogue record of this book is available from the British Library.

ISBN 0–7535–0118–X

Designed by Design 23, London
Printed by Mackays, Chatham.

CONTENTS

~ CHAPTER 1 ~

BOSSES, SECRETARIES AND OFFICE POWER

*The smallest bird can block out the sun if it
perches on your nose.*
Abele Knidelo ~ Twelfth-century Eritrean philosopher

◆

YOUR BOSS
❑ How they got where they are and you didn't

The difference between a boss and a High Street bank is that a bank sometimes gives you credit. Bosses give you things to do and then blame you for doing them. What they never understand is if they didn't give you things to do in the first place, you wouldn't make so many spectacular foul-ups.

Bosses often claim they can do your job standing on their head which is why they generally give the impression of talking through their backside. And of course it goes without saying that no one can do their job better than them, except for their boss. This goes on all the way up the boss ladder right to the Prime Minister where it starts again at the bottom.

Generally, bosses are older than you. If they're not, one of two things must have happened. Either you slept with someone you shouldn't have or they slept with someone you should have slept with. Or else you're very, very dim and have the business talent of a wood shaving.

Bosses love to sign things. In some companies you can't pass wind before getting their signature in triplicate. That doesn't mean they read everything they sign. In fact bosses don't bother reading anything except for your expenses, which they send off to forensic laboratory for detailed analysis.

To be fair bosses have an awful lot of responsibility, which is why they often say 'the buck stops here'. This is an American expression meaning, 'The vast majority of the payroll stops in my wallet'. Bosses also have a number of perks and the bigger the boss they are the bigger the perk is – from company car to big company car to chauffeur-driven car, right through to 'I think I'll work at home'.

7

Naturally there are good bosses and bad bosses. Some take the trouble to get interested in what you are doing, encourage your personal development and generally provide you with a stimulating and challenging environment in which to work. There are also good bosses who lock themselves in their room, have five-hour lunches and leave you completely alone.

KEY LEARNINGS
- **Treat bosses with the respect they think they deserve**
- **Leading from the front doesn't mean from over the horizon**
- **Boss and stud are only synonyms in the Thesaurus**

POWER
❑ To your elbow and other useful places

Power in business is measured by how quickly you could ruin the company if you set your mind to it. Human Resource Departments are dedicated to doing nothing else and yet most companies seem to continue fairly happily despite their best efforts; Human Resource power rating therefore equals zero.

There are two types of power in business. The first is the power to make things happen, launch new ventures and have fun. Approximately one person per company has this power and they are right at the top with the fat pay packet and wide grin. The second type of power is to say no to people and make their lives a misery. This power is widespread and it is the aim of every middle manager to have more people to say no to than can say no to him.

If you're ever in a meeting and bizarre things are happening that have nothing to do with the business in hand, there's probably a power game going on. Men like nothing better than what they call 'a titanic board room struggle on fundamental strategy'. Women have a more accurate term for this sort of behaviour – willy waving.

In business the power you have doesn't equate to your salary. For example the post room can cripple a company for weeks just for a laugh. The cash flow problems of many companies can usually be traced to someone in the post room wedging all the incoming cheques under a desk leg to stop the desk rocking when he puts his head on it to get some sleep.

Nowadays everyone in business is empowered but some are more empowered than others. Jobs with no power feel like travelling on the top front seat of a double decker bus. You can see where you're going but you've got no control and if you hit a low bridge you'll be the first to get it in the neck.

True empowerment is when you decide what you want to do and when you want to do it. In fact it's remarkably like being unemployed and may in fact be a company ruse to prepare you for imminent redundancy. In your best interests you should therefore vigorously resist being empowered at all times.

KEY LEARNINGS
- **Power corrupts**
- **Empowerment corrupts the empowered**
- **Corruption empowers the powerless**

Q&A¹
POWER HUNGRY?
Check your ambition rating

1   If you have a dripping tap at home what are you most likely to do:

A   Turn the radio up
B   Tinker with it yourself and flood the entire house
C   Get a 24-hour plumbing service in within the hour
D   Move house

2   How do you view your current boss?

A   Not quite sure who it is
B   Someone to respect and admire
C   Temporary obstruction
D   Through the cross hairs of a sniper's rifle

3   What would you be happy with in life?

A   Mother of all spliffs
B   My health, my family and regular bowel movements
C   Several million, four houses, Aston Martin, string of polo ponies
D   Immortality

4 During party games do you normally . . .

A Not understand the rules
B Have great fun but get knocked out in the first round
C Cheat, win at all costs and lose all your friends
D Encourage a drug-crazed orgy designed to satisfy your every whim

5 What is your idea of relaxation?

A Four-day LSD trip
B Vigorous game of ping pong followed by a cool Tizer
C Going to work on the weekend and reading other people's mail
D Dressing up as Napoleon and directing trolley traffic in the supermarket

6 What do you think the secret of great leadership is?

A Leaving me well out of it
B A large stomach and a slim briefcase
C I know exactly what it is but I'm keeping it to myself
D Waking up with destiny at your shoulder

7 How powerful would you like to be?

A Powerful enough to get out of this sofa and roll a joint
B Powerful enough to be able to help other people in need
C Powerful enough to do what I want, when I want, to whom I want
D Cruella de Ville, General Schwarzkopf and Vlad the Impaler all rolled into one

8 Would you like to be empowered?

A I'd rather be magic mushroom powered
B If that's OK by everyone else
C I'd rather have the money, car and big house thank you
D My job is to empower the downtrodden masses

9 How far up the corporate ladder do you want to go?

A Just high enough to see where I left my stash
B A little bit higher if there's room or someone dies

C   I'll take the high speed corporate lift if you don't mind
D   Ladders are for tights

10   Do you think power corrupts?

A   Absolutely
B   I shouldn't think so if you're sensible
C   I'm banking on it
D   It does for most people so I better look after it all

Mostly As

You have reached a state of chemical-induced nirvana where power for you or anybody else is a drag. Speaking of which, pass that ganja. You will do well in the post room or advertising.

Mostly Bs

You wouldn't mind a little bit of power as long as there's enough to go round and you can take it back if you don't like it. If you're not already in Personnel you should be.

Mostly Cs

You are a normal executive with healthy ambition and an eye for the main chance. You like working with other people and using their heads to step on on your way up.

Mostly Ds

You show a real aptitude for dressing up, self-aggrandisement and ethnic cleansing. Within a few years you should either be a managing director or sitting on a park bench drinking Special Brew and shouting at people.

THE CHAIRMAN
❑ Proof of life after death

At the top of every company there is a frightening mythical beast called the Chairman. They exist so far above the rest of the company that no one can actually see what they're doing. Which is lucky for them.

The Chairman has to do one day's proper work per year and that is to deliver the annual report and accounts at the Annual General Meeting and speak to the shareholders or 'slum dwellers' as they are known in industry. The night before the AGM, the Chairman will burn the midnight oil thumbing through the Bumper Book of Platitudes. Their big favourite is that 'share prices can go down as well as up', an immutable financial law which doesn't seem to apply to their salary.

Chairmen all model themselves on Prince Charles. They wear beautifully tailored suits and make a point of speaking to grubby worker types so that they can keep in touch with 'the people'. Chairmen are also good for high level soothing, so that when the factory burns down spreading toxic waste over half of Europe, they can soothingly tell everyone that up until the 'minor incident' the company had an excellent safety record and that there's really no need to worry because there will be an immediate independent inquiry chaired by one of their closest friends.

Physically the role of Chairman can be debilitating. Muscular control is the first thing to go and many chairmen find that they can no longer drive and have to be driven everywhere in a large car. Control over their writing also goes until their signature resembles an emergency landing by an ink fly. Most serious of all is that they find it impossible to use any form of self-service restaurant and have to eat in restaurants where they are waited on hand, foot and gullet.

Chairmen also manage relations with the City. If you're making armfuls of cash the City likes you and if you're not the City makes sure you get shat on from a great height.

IT'S WHAT I CALL A 'HANDS ON' APPROACH TO BUSINESS

Maintaining this difficult and sensitive relationship therefore requires a rigorous and sustained programme of lunching. A thin Chairman is therefore a sure sign of a company on its way to the receivers. Chairmen are also noted for their strategic vision. After a particularly good lunch a top-flight Chairman may even experience double vision.

Chairmen often give the impression that they're engaged in matters so lofty that they're simply beyond our comprehension. In fact their day is spent responding to letters that get written to the Chairman of the company by little people who have a piffling problem that customer service departments simply can't be arsed with. If truth be known Chairmen are just big corporate Father Christmases helping little old ladies out with their washers by putting a rocket under middle managers in Macclesfield.

KEY LEARNINGS
- **Chairmen are reassuring and comforting figures**
- **Their job is to produce reassuring and comforting figures for the City**
- **As opposed to reassuring and comforting figurines for your mantel piece**

THE MANAGING DIRECTOR'S OFFICE
❏ Room to manoeuvre

The Managing Director's office is a glorified changing room for the golf course and a quiet sanctuary where they can recover from working breakfasts, lunches, cocktails etc. In the centre of their office they usually have a desk so large you can see the curvature of the earth along the edge of it. Why they need a desk this big is a mystery because they only ever have one piece of paper on it and that piece of paper usually says, 'Remember to go to lunch'. In old-style offices the MD has a little buzzer that summons the secretary. Truly efficient secretaries will anticipate the slightest whim of their boss, will know exactly when the buzzer is going to ring, and will make sure they are away from their desk at that exact moment.

You can tell a lot about the health of a company by the paintings on the walls of the Managing Director's office. If they are original oils from the classical school of eighteenth-century France, then you'll know why the company can only afford to pay you the minimum wage. If, on the other hand, they are original oils from Hannah and Edward of the late twentieth-century Blenheim Road Infants School, then your Managing Director is probably just a big softie. If there is a dead sheep in a glass case in the office, this is either a piece of contemporary art or the Director of Human Resources.

One of the benefits of being the Managing Director is that your office has the best view in the whole building. In some tall office blocks you can spend hours just looking at the view, until it's time to leave for lunch or golf or a massage. Of course Managing Directors need all this space and quiet because in all fairness they have to do a lot of top level strategic thinking. Everyone knows how it's impossible to think straight when the phone is ringing, when four people want to see you and when someone at the next desk is doing Elvis impressions – because everyone, bar the MD, has to do it.

KEY LEARNINGS
- **Ninety-eight per cent of working people have never seen the inside of an MD's office**
- **Thirty-eight per cent of MDs have never seen the inside of an MD's office**
- **Twenty-three per cent of surgeons have never seen the inside of an MD**

SENIOR SECRETARIES
❏ Managing the managers

There are two types of Managing Director's secretary. Firstly there are those resting between modelling assignments who have the typing speed of a one-fingered sloth with a hangover and who get a new car every time they take dictation. Then there are the second sort whose typing makes the teleprinter look like a case of writer's block. They generally wear tweed skirts and combat boots and run the company single handed while the Managing Director is interviewing for her replacement by the first sort. The first sort last for anything up to nine months while the second sort only leave their desks if accompanied by officers of the bomb disposal squad.

The Managing Director's secretary got used to saying no in her late teens and never got out of the habit. The only time she says 'yes' is when you ask her if the Managing Director's diary is completely full for the next three years. If you want to get ahead in the office you must make sure you are in her good books by remembering to buy her presents on key days such as Christmas, her birthday and the anniversary of her wart removal. Things that go down well are Blakeys for her boots, the mature woman's make-over kit from Ronseal and proposals of marriage.

At the Christmas party the lads in the post room often have a bit of a laugh daring each other to dance with her. If you accept the dare it's worth remembering that she uses the same stuff to keep her hair in place as they do to keep water out of the Channel Tunnel. It's therefore not a good idea to run your fingers through her hair in a casual way unless you want to spend the rest of the evening having your hand cut free by the fire brigade.

Always remember that she is the only person in the whole company who is allowed to call the Managing Director a blithering fathead. And if you're the blithering fathead who gets called to see the Managing Director, make sure you get up to his office immediately.

KEY LEARNINGS
- **Powerful organisations need powerful organisation**
- **Maximum-hold hairspray can hold small companies together**
- **Never ask a woman between 48 and 52 how old she is**

Ten things the Managing Director's secretary can do that other secretaries can't
1 Accidentally downsize organisations
2 Reconcile expenses claims worth more than the GNP of Luxembourg
3 Be polite to Managing Director's wife while being on top of the Managing Director
4 Staple Annual Reports with her knees
5 Smoke 40 Capstan full strength before breakfast
6 Stop lift doors closing with her perm
7 Use a staple gun on junior brand manager's genitals
8 Organise vital business travel to coincide with pro-golf tour
9 Drink shop stewards under the table
10 Blow perfect corporate logo in smoke ring

UPWARD MANAGEMENT

❏ Gerbil training

Given the number of colossal fatheads who exist in the world at any given time, there is statistically a very good chance that your boss will also be a colossal fathead. Unless you want the inscription on your tombstone to be 'He worked for a fathead', you will have to find a way of working around your boss and reducing their impact. The term for this is 'upward management.'

In getting round your boss never underestimate the power of gratuitous flattery. If you can fake sincerity, you can get away with 'That's a beautiful pair of grey shoes Mr Dunne, and Velcro fasteners are so practical.' Once you get into the habit of congratulating your boss on tasks that a monkey with learning difficulties could do blindfold, you can move on to selective flattery where they only get the big Branson/Churchill/Moses comparisons when they do something that's actually in your direct interest.

In business the equivalent of giving your teacher an apple is writing a crucial report for your boss which they can then claim is their own. Don't forget to hide away something in the small print, like an admission to a fetish for dressing up in bubble wrap during love making. When this is discovered during their major presentation, your boss will be forced either to admit that they didn't write the report or that, yes, they are in fact 'Bubble wrap Bertie'.

Advanced upward management is managing your boss's boss so that your own boss finds his levers of power strangely useless. There is no limit to how high you can reach with this upward management. Theoretically great upward managers could run a company from the post room. In fact it's remarkable how many apparently insignificant post room workers claim to be doing exactly that.

KEY LEARNINGS
- **Major companies are run from their post room**
- **Your boss is as powerless as you are**
- **Why not suggest your boss moves to the post room**

MIDDLE MANAGERS
❑ **Unleashing the power within to boil a small egg**

SOME PEOPLE CAN MANAGE AND SOME CAN'T. MIDDLE MANAGERS ARE INBETWEEN

In business some people can manage and some people can't. Those in between are called middle managers. The accepted industry definition of a middle manager is somebody who can't quite manage.

No one is more exposed in the corporate hierarchy than the middle manager, because they are neither thinking nor doing. Instead they are interpreting the thoughts of those that think into actions for those that act. In this they serve as corporate magicians where the right thoughts mysteriously become the wrong actions.

It is strange but true that there are one or two people who have wanted to be middle managers ever since they were two, and now that they're shimmering around in their shiny little suits, it's all a dream come true. These are the sort of men who will phone ahead to reserve a table at Little Chefs and who have masonic handshakes so bizarre that when you encounter one it feels like you've grabbed a handful of live whitebait.

Nevertheless, some middle managers are needed in business to do tasks too simple for a computer. Eventually even middle managers latch on to the fact that they have been doing exactly the same job for twen-

THIS COMPANY IS GOING PLACES. I'LL WAIT TILL IT COMES BACK

ty years, so they have to be given promotions to a grade one hair's breadth above their current one and given another letter to put at the end of their Vauxhall Vectra GSXIL.

All middle managers have two recurring nightmares. The first is that their job will be lost to delayering and they will have to set up a hamburger stand in a lay-by as this would require a modicum of initiative and a grasp of basic business principles. The second is that they will be promoted to senior management and will have to start again at the bottom with a Vauxhall Omega L.

KEY LEARNINGS
- Middle management is an anagram for 'mental age of ten'
- Middle management is an anagram for 'dull muddled menial'
- Middle management is an anagram for 'dead mad gentleman'

Ten small steps to middle management mediocrity

1   Invest a small amount of money in grey shoes
2   Banish cotton from your wardrobe
3   Grow a beard without a moustache
4   Never make a phone call when a meeting will do
5   Never finish a meeting while people are still interested or motivated
6   Invite your boss round for Sunday lunch with your naturist vegan wife
7   Attend vital industry seminars three times a week
8   Wear paraffin-based aftershave
9   Hire attractive secretary who turns out to be a man
10 Hire expensive consultants to turn computer on

Top ten middle management films

1   Ted and Gary's Excellent Adventure
2   The Man in the Grey Nylon Suit
3   The Big Sleep
4   Partial Recall
5   Clarks Commando
6   Terminated Contract
7   Last Exit to Swindon
8   Desperately Seeking Promotion
9   The Good, the Bad and the Mediocre
10 The Fall Guy

SECRETARIES
❏ The source of real corporate power

I f you put all the country's Chief Executives in one room, all they would produce would be a range of jammy share options for themselves and some booming corporate waffle for the City. Give them one good secretary and they might get some useful work done. That's why it's very difficult for secretaries to become managers. It's not that secretaries couldn't do management jobs, it's because management couldn't do management jobs without secretaries.

If information is power, then secretaries are the national grid of the corporate world. Secretaries are especially adept at using the phone to control people, information and power. In some cases it's because they are on the phone to their boyfriend for so long that everything else grinds to a complete halt. Good secretaries on the other hand have the ability to shield their bosses so effectively from phone calls and unwanted meetings that they might have died five years ago and no one would be any the wiser. Often an experienced secretary will lock their boss's door from nine to five and tell everyone they cannot be disturbed because they are in 'strategic planning'. Meanwhile the boss is sitting in their room wondering why the door is locked and their phone is dead.

Many of the traditional functions of the secretary are dying out. For example expertise in biscuit preference is a thing of the past. These days if a boss specifies what type of biscuit they want, the likely response from a secretary is, 'And which orifice would you like it shoved in?' These developments leave secretaries with more time to do what they do best – running the business.

KEY LEARNINGS
- **Remember, all confidential memos are typed by secretaries**
- **If you want to know what's really going on in a company ask a secretary**
- **For every senior executive on the golf course there is a junior secretary running a major company**

STEREOTYPING
❏ Should secretaries work with the radio on?

There is often a bit of rivalry in the office between secretaries about their typing speeds. There is always one in every office who claims to do 120 wpm. Amazingly this is always the secretary who has nails that would give a sabre-toothed tiger the willies. In actual fact they can type at this speed but when you read what comes out it has so many typos it looks like the first verse of the Polish national anthem. You'll also notice that secretaries who claim to do over 100 wpm are also the same secretaries that do 10 mwpd which stands for 10 minutes work per day.

Secretaries have many weird and wonderful abilities. One of them is being able to type lengthy documents without a single typo but not having the first idea what it's about. Another ability is that of signing letters from their bosses in their absence. This can be quite worrying when you look closely at something like the Declaration of Independence and discover that many of the signatures actually read something like: Clare Howe p.p. George Washington.

There is an increasing demand for graphologists in business. These are people who analyse handwriting and make character references from it. Secretaries have been doing this unpaid for years, deciphering writing that looks like the death crawl of a haemorrhaging fly, and making an instant analysis that the writer is a total pain in the arse.

For people who are used to word processors, it is one of the wonders of the world how secretaries in the past managed to work with manual typewriters. Typing a capital P meant lifting the equivalent of eighteen pounds dead-weight with your little finger and typing the average letter was the aerobic equivalent of an hour on the bench press. No wonder most men left the profession to relax in the construction industry.

KEY LEARNINGS
- **Keyboard skills should not be mistaken for emery board skills**
- **No women born after 1964 take dictation in the office or anywhere else thank you**
- **Voice recognition systems still refuse to listen to IT directors**

Words when typed most likely to break secretaries' nails

Xylophone	Floccinancinhilipilification
Eschscholtzia	You're sacked, Miss Meakin

~ CHAPTER 2 ~

MONEY, POSITION
AND PROMOTION

*When one door closes,
make sure you've got your foot in it*
Paul Arongani ~ Nineteenth-century Fijian poet and pharmacist

RECRUITMENT
❑ Picking on someone your own size

One of the reasons so many people work in offices is because they apply for jobs that say 'Executive Opportunity' when what they offer is 'Series of Irritating Chores'.

When people look at a job ad the first thing they look at is the salary. That's why you can advertise for a Chief Executive at 100K and get a pack of plumbers, carpet fitters and assistant librarians applying. The next thing they look at is the location. If it's Swindon the salary could be 500K and you'd still only get a trickle of interest from industrial archaeologists and the local unemployed. Salaries of 'up to 45K' mean that's what you'll get if you agree to take a cut from 60K. Otherwise it's 30K.

Pay no attention to the job description unless it's something incredibly specific like stonemason or ship broker. Ignore anything that has words like fast moving, marketing, executive, people focused, etc. They're all shorthand for double glazing salesman on 9K basic with commission. 'All the usual benefits' means cramped office, rotting carpets, vending machine coffee, crippling work load, bastard for a boss, hormonal secretary and swingeing headcount reduction every six months. If partying and drugs are still important to you then you're probably wasting your time applying for any job with the word President in it (with the possibly exception of US President).

Size of recruitment ad is important. A full page colour ad in *The Economist* is likely to be more lucrative than a small box ad in your local paper that says 'Earn big money fast', although to hedge your bets it's worth applying for both. A lot of high-level recruitment is done by head-hunters. Like traditional head-hunters, they take your head and, through a process of getting you rejected for a series of low-level jobs, seriously reduce the size of it.

KEY LEARNINGS
- **Every job advertised has driven the previous occupant to resignation or suicide**
- **Good jobs are never advertised**
- **Because people keep them to themselves and close friends**

YOU'VE PUT UNDER YOUR INTERESTS, 'CANNIBALISM'. CAN YOU TELL ME A LITTLE BIT MORE ABOUT THAT, MR. JENKINS?

CVs

❑ The power of creative writing

Everyone has a talent for creative writing, and nowhere is this more in evidence than in CVs. If the people described in CVs actually existed, the business world would be packed with highly educated, multi-lingual, computer-literate, team-playing perfectionists instead of the knackered rabble of clock-watchers you find in real life.

Most CVs can be written with the normal gross exaggeration and good old fashioned lying, but one section needs special care – that marked interests. Do not put down walking or reading as everyone does that and you might as well put down breathing and farting. You should also strenuously avoid giving the impression that you have a seriously interesting life by putting down glamorous things like snow boarding, quad-bike polo and nude bungee jumping. Let's face it, if you do all these sexy, happening things why would you be so interested in a career in sandpaper marketing.

Your educational record should start from the beginning and work forward. But use your common sense. If you've got an MBA from Harvard it won't be necessary to include your two gold stars from Mrs Barlow for your egg carton Stegosaurus. CVs are so packed full of huge porkies that the truth can quite often get you noticed. Try something like: Education – wasted.

Putting down details of your current salary is the ultimate Catch 22 because obviously you want to earn a lot more wonga than you're on now. Again lying through your teeth is the best policy unless you've applied for one of those much sought after jobs at the Inland Revenue.

Never enclose your photo with a CV. Photo booths have a special camera that doubles your chin, thins your hair and crosses your eyes. Make them wait until the interview before they decide they don't like the look of you.

KEY LEARNINGS
- **Write your CV as you would write a letter to Santa**
- **No one has ever been hired because of their interest in karaoke**
- **Never use the phrase 'frottage monster' anywhere in your CV**

INTERVIEW TECHNIQUE
❏ What to do if you haven't got it

Most people who have a job know in their heart of hearts that a monkey could do it equally well. Of course the difficult part of any job is getting it in the first place. That's because of something called a job interview, which is a cross between *Blind Date* and the Spanish Inquisition. Interviews start with the knock on the door, lesson one therefore is to make sure you knock on the right door. Getting all psyched up for the big entrance and then disappearing into the broom cupboard is no way to start a career in high finance.

Once inside the room, the next thing to do is to close the door, but on no account should you turn your back while doing this. If you do, the split second your back is turned is enough for the head of the panel to raise one eyebrow and for the other six members to put a large cross against your name. From then on you could have the CV of Sir John Harvey Jones and still not get the job of post room assistant.

The next vital thing to do is to avoid sitting down. If you have watched any television at all, you'll know that really top business people take off their jackets and stand, hands clasped behind their back, staring out of the window in a visionary kind of way. So, hang your jacket on the chair and make for that window. If they don't offer you the job on the strength of that, then they're not the creative, happening company that deserve to have you.

If you must sit down try taking the chair and pulling it right up to the desk where the interviewer is sitting. They will instinctively move their own chair back and then they will be the one sitting in the lonely chair in the middle of nowhere. From this point on you're in charge. Ask them probing questions about their job and finish off with 'but surely a monkey could do that'.

KEY LEARNINGS
- **Never fart audibly in an interview unless it's part of the job description**
- **Bringing your six poorly dressed, malnourished children to the interview cuts no ice in the financial sector**
- **You can only pass on three questions in any one interview**

Five great interview questions for cutting interview candidates down to size

1   What's the capital of Bolivia?
2   If I have three apples and I don't give you any, why do you think that is?
3   How would you rightsize a matrix management structure while implementing TQM from an empowered stakeholder base?
4   If you're so brilliant why haven't you got a decent job already?
5   You've said your interests are chess and walking. They're not very interesting, are they?

RESIGNATION
❏ Immediate self-disempowerment

There are many ways of leaving your job. By far the easiest is death because it cuts out the P45, the clearing your desk and the embarrassing leaving party.

Telling your boss that you're leaving the company is difficult because it tends to confirm all the bad things they've thought about you all along. Try using the language they would use if they were sacking you: 'I'm afraid you're going to have to let me go,' or 'I'm streamlining my operation and I'm afraid this company has no part in it'. When you've finished that, don't forget to add for good measure, 'And I wouldn't piss on you if you were on fire, you rancid old crook.'

If you're the sort of person who loses their temper very quickly, whatever you do, fight against the temptation to say, 'I resign!' Bosses these days are like vultures constantly wheeling round in search of a voluntary redundancy and you'll be out of the door before you can say, 'Of course, I was joking, sir'. To put things in their proper perspective, throw all your money and credit cards in the bin because that's basically what'll happen if you don't keep your big mouth shut.

You certainly find out who your friends are when you resign. Generally they're the people you went to Primary School with and who will still be your friends where you're in an old people's home. The people at work will think you're the bravest, coolest and most strong-minded individual, in recognition of which they will avoid all eye contact and never speak to you again.

You'll know how well you've done in the company by the leaving bash they put on for you. If it's a Brown Derby at the Wimpy with Rob from accounts then you should have left years ago. If it's a champagne reception with no expense spared, you're either going to be a rich source of business in your new job or the whole company is incredibly happy that you're leaving.

Leaving gifts should really be called parting shots. When your boss says, 'We've had a whip round and we've bought you this pack of Refreshers', it's very difficult to take out a positive message about your standing in the office. On the other hand if your parting gift is a voucher at the Citizens' Advice Bureau, you'd better watch out for a heavyweight breach of contract suit coming your way.

The process of clearing your desk gives you a very good indication of the reasons you are leaving. If there is nothing on your desk, you're probably leaving because you are going to a bigger and better job and you have pilfered everything from your company that can be moved physically or electronically. However, if your desk has been completely clear for the last three years of employment it may be that you are completely surplus to company requirements or work in PR or both. Conversely, if clearing your desk is the hardest work you've done since you joined the company, you might be leaving because there is no longer any room on your desk to store untouched work.

KEY LEARNINGS
- **When one door shuts another door slams in your face**
- **It's always darkest before it's absolutely pitch black**
- **The light at the end of the tunnel is on a time switch**

APPRAISALS
❑ The truth hurts

Appraisals are when you get together with your team leader and agree what an outstanding member of the team you are, how much your contribution has been valued, what massive potential you have and, in recognition of all this, would you mind having your salary halved.

Appraisals happen once a year, usually the week after you caused millions of pounds worth of damage by spilling your coffee into the mainframe computer. Remember, there is no room for humour in appraisals. In the box marked 'How would you rate your teamwork skills?' avoid putting, 'A lot higher than those other bastards'. Don't forget that body language is also important. Starting your appraisal on both knees with your hands clasped in prayer and sobbing loudly may be read as lack of confidence.

Some companies go in for something called self-appraisal. This doesn't mean a couple of hours in front of the mirror saying, 'Tony-boy, you are the dog's bollocks.' It actually means taking a long hard look at all your strengths and weaknesses and then ignoring all your weaknesses except for your 'obsessive drive for perfection'.

We've all been brought up not to lie, but this obviously doesn't apply to appraisals. You lied through your teeth to get the job so there's no point getting all honest six months later. The best approach is a balance between cringing apology and grovelling sycophancy, something like: 'My respect for you is so intense that it sometimes distracted me thereby causing the continual string of major cock-ups which have been the main feature of my performance this year.'

Giving appraisals is as hard as getting them. The secret is to mix criticism with recognition. For example; 'You've made a number of mistakes Martin, but we recognise that you made them because you're a total idiot.'

KEY LEARNINGS
- **Appraisals are the fairground mirrors of performance**
- **Appraisals are where 'praise' comes between 'appals'**
- **Appraisals are the ladders in the tights of your career**

Appraisals – what they say	What they mean
'Hello Martin'	'You're fired'
'Please have a seat'	'You're going to need it'
'So how are things going generally?'	'When can you clear your desk?'
'How have I managed you in the last year, Martin?'	'Last chance to make brownie points, Martin'
'This year we've got some stretching targets'	'Last year you did nothing'
'Let's talk about salary for a moment'	'Talk's all you'll get'
'You need to network more'	'Here's a Network SE timetable'
'Just between us, Martin'	'I'm gay'
'How's life outside work'	'Are you gay?'
'You need to develop yourself personally'	'I can sell you steroids'
'We must work more closely, Martin'	'I love you Martin'
'How do you see your future in the company?'	'Undress and lie on the sofa'

PROMOTION
❏ Getting what others deserve before they do

Getting a promotion at work has strange physical side-effects. Firstly it changes your eyesight so you suddenly see what a load of good-for-nothing shirkers the rest of your team are. It also lengthens your wind so that you take up ten per cent more air time in meetings. After getting a promotion most people try and prove they deserve it by becoming Business Nazi of the Year for the next three months until they run out of steam or are swiftly demoted again.

Not all promotions are on merit. You can get ahead by sleeping with the right people or just abject crawling. Of course you can try abject crawling while sleeping with someone, but be careful that you don't end up coming into the office in a leather face mask that you can't get off. There is another form of promotion where you can go from greasy-faced, grey-shoed middle manager to sleek-cheeked fat cat overnight. This is called privatisation.

Promotion should never be confused with self-promotion. This is where you spend so much time telling everyone just how wonderful you are, that eventually the company decides that it simply doesn't deserve to keep you. Also don't confuse promotion with sales promotion. This is where smiling, lizard-like wide boys promise to promote your company to the status of global mega-brand by stamping your logo on a plastic key ring.

You know when you've had a really good promotion when you can afford to have another child. Sadly, you won't have time to conceive it until you're recovering from your stress-induced mental breakdown. It's not a promotion if you have to send the children you already have down the mines to pay the mortgage. Never, ever fall for the line, 'We're giving you a big promotion, but your salary will remain the same'. It's exactly the same as, 'I really like you, but not in that way'.

KEY LEARNINGS

- If you're promoted three times in the same year and you still have the same boss, something fishy is going on
- People are promoted to one level below the competence of their boss
- Never ask for a promotion from someone who is only one step ahead of you

---

MONEY
❏ Apparently it doesn't grow on trees

Money talks and what it usually says is 'spend me'. That's why it's impossible to hear the words 'pay day' and not feel a sudden desire to go shopping. The reason why people work a five-day week and have a two-day weekend is that you can generally spend money twice as fast as you make it. In fact the less you earn the more you shop, which explains why shops are always clogged up with kids, pensioners and utter wastrels. Shopping wouldn't be the same if things were labelled with the time you had to work to earn the money for them. That blouse might not look quite so irresistible if it was labelled, 'two days' work plus two hours' overtime'.

Companies often have mission statements stuck up on the wall explaining why they're in business. If their employees had their own mission statements on the wall, most of them would say, 'I need the money'. Of course if someone paid you a nice salary to lie in bed all day picking your navel then we'd all be in advertising.

On pay day you can almost hear your bank account sighing with relief. Sadly your bank account doesn't know about your credit card statement itemising how you spent this month's salary last month.

What you get paid is shown on your pay slip. They're called pay slips because after all the deductions your pay slips dramatically. Tax is the worst. You're taxed when you earn money, when you spend money and when you save money. The only way to avoid tax is to stand very still until you die. (Even then you get clobbered by death duties.) And then there's National Insurance contributions, which don't even have a no-claims bonus. Finally there are your pension contributions which give you money when you're old so that you can keep on paying taxes until you finally make it to the big tax haven in the sky.

The most closely guarded secret in the office is what everyone else earns and that's why human resource people are so smug because they all know just what you're on and give the impression that everyone else on your level is actually being paid far, far more. What really hurts is that it's probably true.

KEY LEARNINGS
- Money can't buy you love
- It used to be able to
- But that's inflation for you

Q&A2 MONEY
how much does it mean to you?

1   How much money do you currently have?

A   Enough for the bus fare home and a bag of chips
B   Enough to get within a week or so of pay day
C   A substantial chunk of capital in a broad portfolio of investments
D   Why ask about money when there are flowers to smell

2   If you won £1,000,000 on the lottery what would you do with it?

A   I would blow it on houses, cars, drugs and end up in prison
B   Pay off my credit cards, buy mum a house, give some to charity

C   Invest in a broad range of investments to get good investment income

D   What's a million pounds compared to dappled sunlight in a spring wood?

3   What are the typical contents of your wallet/purse?

A   Betting slip, pawn broker's slip, bailiff's calling card, one Irish punt

B   £15 cash, eighteen store cards, four supermarket loyalty cards, three kidney donor cards

C   More gold cards than King Midas's Christmas post bag

D   Dried rosemary, druid's incantation, various crystals

4   When shopping how do you usually pay?

A   In prison for shoplifting

B   Credit at eye-watering interest rates

C   Shopping is a drain on valuable investment income and to be avoided

D   Barter and occasional begging backed up with voodoo curses

5   What can't money buy you?

A   Taste

B   Enough clothes

C   A personality

D   Enlightenment

6   A group of you arrive in a pub together. Do you . . .

A   Say 'mine's a large one' and disappear to the loo

B   Say 'what are you having' and check whether they take credit cards

C   Open a tab and have the locals secretly drinking themselves blind on it

D   Get your divining rod out and volunteer to locate beer if someone pays for it

7   What's the biggest overdraft you've ever had?

A   About £520 cash and various child support stuff
B   No overdraft but owe about £75,000 on store cards
C   £10.50 when a student after bank admin cock-up. Sued
      bank for half a million
D   About £1.2 billion when Chief Executive of nationalised
   industry

8   Could you live without money?

A   I do
B   If I had one Gold card
C   Money I can live without as long as I maintain the value of
   my investments
D   Could money live without us?

**9   Would you ever consider having a partner poorer
      than you?**

A   Restricts the field somewhat
B   As long as their credit was good
C   Excellent tax advantages in doing so
D   When someone is rich in spirit what matter if they are low
      on readies

10   Is money the root of all evil?

A   I don't know but I'd like to find out
B   Yes and therefore it should be spent as quickly as you
      get it
C   Not in certain off-shore locations
D   I have dug for many roots and never found money

Mostly As

You love money but unfortunately it is an unrequited love. You spend most of your time waving goodbye to money as it disappears somewhere else at a frightening rate. Your credit rating is one of the lowest in the developed world.

Mostly Bs

You like spending money and you have the wardrobe, car accessories and soft furnishings to prove it. You also have credit card statements that look like a transcription of the entire Argos catalogue. You owe your soul to Mastercard.

Mostly Cs

You can't remember the last time you spent money and you'd be hard pressed to describe what cash looked like. You are worth many hundreds of thousands of pounds in investments so secure and so long-term that you are actually living in crushing poverty.

Mostly Ds

You obviously made a vast amount of money in the sixties through fashion or advertising or LSD. Since then you've been making big efforts to prove that money isn't important to you and you are willing to spend thousands to prove it.

YOUR PACKAGE
❑ Yes, size is important

Possibly the smallest and most intense source of pleasure in the world, apart from the you-know-what, is the pay packet. Nothing is more satisfying than being given a little brown envelope full of the folding stuff, especially if the folding stuff happens to be cash. Pay packets are traditionally given out on Friday because if they gave them out on Monday no one would come to work on Tuesday or Wednesday.

In the old days men used to take their pay packets home, give them straight to their wives and be given a few pence back for beer. Today nothing has changed except that men now give ninety per cent of their earnings straight to the Child Support Agency leaving a few quid which is then handed straight over to the Inland Revenue.

There are many different ways of getting paid. If you have to crawl into your boss's office on your knees and your money is then thrown on the floor, you should be aware that this is not the normal way to get paid. These days computer payslips have taken over from the pay packet and all you get is a little printout that shows you what you would have earned before it was all deducted for tax, National Insurance, pension, mortgage and the national debt. If you're in a hurry and you want to find out quickly how much you've actually got to spend, look for the smallest figure on the whole slip. That's yours. Don't spend it all at once.

Around about Christmas time the prospect of a bonus becomes very important, especially once you've already spent twice what you hope to be getting. Naturally this is when you're told that this year, instead of getting a bonus, you will be put on performance-related pay. This is where they give you a pitifully insulting pay packet and, if you make a performance, they take it all back.

KEY LEARNINGS
- No one is paid what they think they're worth
- Just be grateful you're not paid what you're really worth
- They're called deductions because you need to be Sherlock Holmes to work out what they're for

---

NEGOTIATION
❏ Ask for the earth and get it!

In business everything is negotiable, including your salary. However, before you run off and start horse trading with your boss, remember that negotiation can mean things go down as well as up and that you might come out of a very invigorating three-hour negotiation with your salary halved, your pension stopped and your company car downgraded to a pair of roller blades.

Many books have been written about the art of negotiation, with titles such as, *Getting to Yes*. Most ordinary people would probably be better off with one called, *Getting to You Must Be Joking*. If you're ever thinking of writing a book about negotiation, don't. Anyone that reads it properly will naturally take it back to the shop and demand their money back for some completely spurious reason.

There are three basics of negotiation (but for you I can do four). Firstly, remember that negotiation is all just a game, like rugby for example; you go head to head with some ugly bruiser, push like a nutter and someone else gets the ball. Secondly, go in high. If they accept your first figure and you still feel cheated, it wasn't high enough. Finally, you must always negotiate knowing what you want to get out at the end. There's no point haggling with a cab driver to get you home if the conclusion is that the price is slashed but you end up going to his home.

Never negotiate with double glazing salesmen. They should be dealt immediate and crushing pain as an opening position and then you should back this up by a philosophical demolition of their very existence, a religious warning of their eternal damnation and a historical assault against their social and family background. The final golden rule is that you've lost the negotiation if it ever gets personal. Which is why divorces are the most traumatic, agonising and expensive negotiations outside the plumbing trade.

KEY LEARNINGS
- **Go in high**
- **Hit low**
- **Bite, scratch and gouge**

PERKS

❏ Use them or lose them

Perks are so called because when you have one they make you feel perky. If you think your job has a perk but in fact it makes you feel intensely depressed then you may be confusing a business perk with an occupational hazard. Beware of any perks that include the phrase 'all you can eat', especially if you work in heavy engineering.

The top management perk is travel. A three-day, all expenses paid trip to see a new production facility in Thailand is to all intents and purposes a holiday and has the added spice of being done on full pay. The non-management equivalent of this is the sickie, where people decide that they worked hard enough the day before to spend a day under the duvet, out shopping and generally swanning about in their dressing gown. This of course has the added spice of being done on full pay. It's a rum fact that many of these sickies tend to coincide with management trips to Thailand.

Perks vary from job to job. If you are a dustman you might pick up the odd unwanted doll which you then strap to the radiator grill of your lorry. Along similar lines, people in PR might get to bonk a minor royal and then spill the beans to *Hello!* For the millions of people who work in front of computer screens, perks are limited to computer games of sickening depravity and the chance to hack into the accounts department and adjust the decimal point on your salary.

Of course some people take perks too far: timber yard workers taking 'offcuts' to construct a Swiss style chalet in their back garden; estate agents who 'house sit' a stately home for the summer; car mechanics who 'roadtest' your Aston Martin for a week in Wales; accountants who take home a pencil for 'sharpening'.

KEY LEARNINGS
- Perks are croutons in the soup of life
- They're only burnt bits of toast
- But they make the soup seem more of a meal

EXPENSES
❏ Making ends overlap

Expenses are the black economy of the white-collar world. Huge creative and financial energy is dedicated to the expense claim, or 'non-taxable bonus' as it is also known. Doing the boss's expenses is a combination of money laundering and creative accounting and any secretary interested in the possibilities of blackmail need only photocopy their boss's expense claim and threaten to send it to their spouse, the Managing Director, the Inland Revenue or all three. Secretaries have their own form of expenses called petty cash, although Finance Directors often find it hard to see just what's so petty about $300 cash spent on 'Brad Pitt calendar and other merchandise for staff welfare'.

Cabbies know all about fiddling expenses and if you give them a particularly generous tip they will often give you a whole wad of receipts for you to fill out at your leisure for huge sums that would represent a taxi fare from one side of Britain to another at bank holiday rates. You can also try this trick when you're flying abroad. Get them to give you a couple of old air tickets and claim that on your flight to Dublin you also had to fly to Mombasa for 'client development'.

There is a time-honoured language used to describe what expenses supposedly cover. Anything that you can eat or drink or gives you an all-over total body massage when you're by yourself is called 'subsistence'. Anything you eat or drink or have rubbed into you when you're with someone else is called 'entertainment'. And anything that you really should have bought for yourself in the shops on Saturday or done in your leisure time on Sunday is called 'new business'. The one thing no one has ever written against an expense claim is, 'probably unnecessary expense, please deduct from my wages'.

LIFE IS A LEGITIMATE BUSINESS EXPENSE

KEY LEARNINGS
- **A love of money is the root of all expenses**
- **Life is a legitimate business expense**
- **I have the receipt therefore I subsist**

Ten great moments in expense claims

Expense	Claim
1 Putting three children through public school	'training'
2 Lifting face four times	'sundries'
3 Failed take-over bid for Midland Bank	'out of pocket expenses'
4 Eight-month globetrotting golfing extravaganza	'export drive'
5 Staging of Wagner's Ring Cycle	'entertainment'
6 Three weeks on Paris–Dakkar rally	'client visit'
7 Feeding of the five thousand	'subsistence'
8 Deforestation of one third of Amazon rainforest	'stationery'
9 Five years' fertility treatment	'child-minding'
10 Two-week LSD trip	'research'

~ CHAPTER 3 ~

SEX, ALCOHOL
AND STRESS

What your heart desires, your liver pays for.
(There's also some involvement by the pancreas)
Michael Costadides ~ Fourteenth-century Cypriot mystic and hypochondriac

OFFICE CRUSHES
❏ Static electricity

There are two types of office crush. One is where you all crowd around the notice board to read an illicit photocopy of a letter from the communicable diseases unit to your boss. The other is far sweeter and that is the crush you have on someone in the office. By crush we don't mean two sweaty bodies crushed in the stationery cupboard grasping each other's buttocks. We mean an innocent, primary school, behind the bike sheds kind of thing.

Crushes lead to odd behaviour. When the birthday card for the object of your crush is passed round and everyone else writes 'Have a great day', you find yourself writing 'How do I love thee, let me count the ways'. The worst time is the Christmas party. It seems that as soon as you get a chance to dance with your sweetheart, the pounding disco music immediately ends and something like 'Come bring me your softness' starts. You get so stirred up that you have to rush back to your desk and cool off with some difficult sales figures.

If you find yourself memorising the number of someone's favourite drink in the vending machine on the off chance that one day you might be able to say 'Of course, you're a 312, whipped black coffee with no sugar, I can tell', then you very probably have a crush on them and you're certainly a sad, sad individual.

39

No one ever develops a crush for anyone who works in the same part of the office because nothing cures a crush faster than overhearing your beloved on the phone detailing the acts of unspeakable depravity they indulged in after getting legless in some meat market wine bar.

The golden rule is never divulge who you have a crush on. This will get back to them quicker than a ping on their knicker elastic and from then on you won't be able to speak to them, work with them or share a lift with them. You might as well resign, or ask them to marry you, whichever seems less frightening.

KEY LEARNINGS
- **When you're found out it's you who gets crushed**
- **The sweeter the crush the more bitter the disappointment**
- **An office crush provides 0.5 per cent of the daily recommended dose of vitamin C**

OFFICE AFFAIRS
❑ Laying your colleague on the table

I f you work in an office there is a good chance that two people within twenty yards are bonking each other's brains out. You'll know who they are because generally they're the ones without brains. Look for the little tell-tale signs like continuous rhythmic grunting from the stationery cupboard, buttock prints on the board room table, or huge Y-fronts draped over the rubber plant.

There is a long and sad tradition of secretaries having affairs with their bosses. This is always a sign of a bad secretary because really good secretaries manage their boss's time so tightly that the thought of an affair wouldn't have time to enter their head let alone any other part of their body.

Appraisals are often a time when hidden tensions bubble up. Key words like interpersonal, performance, and flexibility take on whole new meanings and '360° appraisals' may well be the polite term for seeing your boss in the nude for the first time. Most sex in the office is done with clothes on which is why stockings and suspenders are a big plus for women and one-piece romper suits with Velcro rip flaps are great for men.

Office affairs are more common in some departments than others. In the marketing department, marketing is what you do between various positioning exercises with one of your colleagues on the top of the desk in the 'quiet room'. In the IT department everyone has long since forgotten how to interact with living creatures so affairs generally tend to happen with people from accounts. The Personnel department have long lost any trace of genuine feeling and no one could possibly have sex with someone who smiled all the time and called you by your first name every time they said anything to you.

What betrays most office affairs in the end is that, after the bonking has been done in total silence and in utter secrecy, some people can't resist the urge to have a cigarette and you'll see them standing outside the building, with a faraway look in their eyes, puffing away stark naked.

KEY LEARNINGS
- **Never make love within arm's reach of a staple gun**
- **After making love in the office insist on a contact report**
- **Don't talk about 'downsizing' when you first see a man naked**

Q&A₃ MEN
check your sexual power rating

1   When you say hello to a woman in a bar does she...

A   Start loosening her clothing and reciting her phone number
B   Shake her collection tin harder
C   Turn out to be a man
D   Look up slowly, put down her French novel and start
     smouldering

2   Where do you think the proper place for a woman is?

A   Whatever position is most comfortable
B   On a pedestal
C   I'll check with my girlfriend
D   They have an intuitive understanding of where they are

3   What does foreplay mean to you?

A   The time I spend in front of the mirror before I go out
B   The introduction to Shakespeare
C   The run-up before diving on the bed
D   A thousand tiny kisses with whispered love poetry and
     chocolate nipple painting

**4   When you make love to a woman does she usually
     orgasm?**

A   Difficult to tell with all the screaming, wailing and panting
B   Women can't orgasm can they?
C   She might do when I've finished and gone down the pub
D   It's more intense than an orgasm

5   What is your favourite chat up line?

A   Do you want to come often?
B   We seem to be the only ones left without a partner
C   I am so pissed I could shag a wall
D   I see you're reading Balzac. You know that rhymes with
     scrotal sack

6   Where is your favourite place for making love?

A   The other side of a pair of satin knickers
B   In my bedroom at home with the lights off
C   Basildon
D   Florence when the bees are on the acacia

7   What is your most attractive feature?

A   Personality
B   Conservatory
C   Nob
D   Intuitive sensitivity

8   What are women most likely to say after making love with you?

A   That was the best ever, Trevor
B   Are you sure that's part of aromatherapy?
C   Get off
D   Je t'aime beaucoup, mon chevalier. Maintenant, ouvres la fenêtre

9   When you are on the pull, what underpants do you wear?

A   Banana hammock
B   Thermal long johns with rear cat flap
C   Bart Simpson boxers
D   Black lycra trunks with Velcro Fly

10   What part of a women most turns you on?

A   Hand
B   Apron
C   The lot
D   Soul

Mostly As

You animal you. Let's face it, you are just one big smoking sex monster. If sexual attraction is all in the mind, then no one has a bigger imagination than you.

Mostly Bs

Women are a closed book to you. That's why you spend so much time in the library trying to find one.

Mostly Cs

Women are a fantastic accompaniment to football and beer, especially after a really beery match when you want to wind down quickly and go to sleep.

Mostly Ds

You are a deeply sensitive and caring romantic and you are God's gift to the sort of woman who doesn't mind going out with a total wanker.

BODY LANGUAGE
❏ What are you looking at?

Body language in the office can be divided into two clear messages. The first one is 'I want to get your kit off' and this message is used by men about thirty-five times a day, whenever there is a woman present, in every part of the office on any occasion from a sales meeting to a pencil sharpening. As most men have the sexual sophistication of a small dog, women are fairly safe in assuming that any movement of any kind is a sign of male sexual arousal. Perhaps not surprisingly the other key message in body language is, 'Why don't you get a life, you sad bastard', which is used by women on a semi-permanent basis in the office, at home and in bed.

There is one other piece of office body language you need to watch out for which is 'You are about to be fired'. This can be an extremely subtle sign with the slightest arching of an eyebrow indicating that your career has just ended. Other signs can be less subtle. For example, if your boss gets the rest of your team to strip you naked and feed your extremities to the shredder, this may well signify displeasure on their part for an action on your part. It's all in the interpretation.

Many offices have now introduced voluntary pre-flirting agreements in which both sides waive the right to a lengthy courtroom battle before they whisper remarks to each other such as 'Can I show you my spreadsheets, Miss Sadler.'

Touching in the office is a sexual minefield. Squeezing past someone in the corridor can easily be misinterpreted as attempted penetration and you can find yourself in front of an industrial tribunal before you can say 'Good morning Miss Grimshaw'. Of course all this non-touching and respecting everyone's personal space is forgotten when the whole office is forced to do these ridiculous teambuilding exercises which involve hugging, touching and often full-blown intercourse. The only safe option is to work at home where you can sexually harass yourself to your heart's content.

KEY LEARNINGS
- In the politically correct office, body language has no transitive verbs
- Don't touch a computer unless it has been designated a 'touch screen'
- In Portugal, holding hands with your boss is perfectly acceptable during a sales demonstration

Top ten bits of men women like to look at in the office

1   Eyes
2   Hands
3   Buttocks
4   Hair
5   Clothes
6   Legs
7   Lips
8   Lunch-box
9   Company car
10 Wallet

Top two bits of women men like to look at in the office
Breasts

SEXUAL POLITICS
❑ Who's on top?

These days everyone who walks erect in business accepts that there is no real difference between the sexes and that they're both absolutely equal in terms of talent, professionalism and ambition. In fact this is a myth put about by women to make men feel better about themselves, because in most areas of business, apart from lifting heavy engine blocks, women have men well and truly whipped.

Of course women have many inbuilt advantages in business. Any woman who can run a house full of screaming children will have no trouble participating in board-level discussions. Any woman who has ever warmed a bottle with one hand and changed a nappy with the other will have no difficulty working with an advertising agency. And any woman who has been in continuous labour for eight hours will have no trouble sitting through a presentation from the head of IT.

Nowadays an increasing number of bosses are women and there is no more effective and powerful combination than a female boss and a female secretary working in close harmony. Which is why so many men are very grateful that this so rarely happens.

BELIEVE ME, I'M AS FEMINIST AS THE NEXT MAN

Men and women have very different ways of bonding in the office. Gratuitous compliments about hair and clothing are the entry-level stuff for women. 'Ooh that's a nice blouse' is the female equivalent of 'Did you see the football?' The next level for a man would be, 'What team do you support.' For women the next stage is swapping all the innermost secrets of every relationship they've ever had. True intimacy for top male executives is going to a match together and drinking five times the maximum capacity of their bladders. For top female executives, it's getting business out of the way quickly and efficiently so they can spend the rest of the meeting giggling uncontrollably.

KEY LEARNINGS
- **Working women are a fact of life**
- **Many men are embarrassed by the facts of life**
- **Tough**

BALANCING HOME AND WORK
❏ While someone rocks the tightrope

Nineties women run businesses, raise families, support the arts and have regular thundering orgasms – women call this juggling their lives. When men say they are juggling their lives you can take this to mean a state of continuous balls-up. The only balls men keep in continuous motion are the ones in their pockets.

Juggling is a bit of a circus act and men can't stand the fact that they can't do it as well as women. That's why when women are busy juggling, men try and grab attention with other circus acts such as lion-taming, fire-eating, sword-swallowing and getting shot from the end of a cannon – all in a day's work for your typical male sales executive.

Sometimes juggling so many things at once can be too much to cope with. That's why there is a growing trend towards downshifting. This is a way of re-balancing your life by reducing stress at work and spending more time at home with your family. Sadly, you may find that time spent with your family is actually the cause of stress. If a survey was done at three o'clock in the morning when your screaming baby had just woken you up for the third time, the result would be ninety per cent of executives desperate to spend less time with their families and more time in the office.

Young children are occasionally brought into the office and it can be quite amusing to have them running around the office for about 3.6 seconds. Unfortunately bosses use this as an excuse to bring their own children in who are in their mid-twenties, are given a major department to run, a fat salary and car, and stay for thirty years.

KEY LEARNINGS
- **You can't downshift before you've upshifted**
- **Some people spend all their time upshifting and downshifting**
- **This is called shift work**

Q&A₄ WOMEN
check your sexual power rating

1   When you walk down the street do you turn . . .

A   Heads
B   Stomachs
C   Into every clothes shop
D   Up your trouser legs and sing 'Puppy Love'.

2   When you take your clothes off what reaction do you get?
A   Cheering, clapping, jostling
B   Immediate blackout

C   Shock and embarrassment of other shoppers
D   Photosynthesis

3   When making love in a car what is your favourite position?

A   Both in back seat, chauffeur in front seat
B   In the garage
C   Man in car park, woman in Harvey Nichols
D   Woman in back seat, man in glove compartment

4   How many lovers have you had in the past twenty years?

A   Can count them on five hands and a foot
B   Can count them on one trotter
C   One Dorothy Perkins lingerie department's worth
D   Ask me again in five minutes

5   What do you look for most in a man?

A   Hung like a moose
B   Pulse
C   Wallet
D   Beethoven hairstyle, dark eyes, strong fingers

6   If you only had one accessory in bed what would it be?

A   Leopard skin body stocking with ejectable gusset
B   Wedding ring
C   Gold Card
D   Branding iron

7   During sex what's most likely to be going through your mind?

A   Keanu Reeves
B   National Anthem
C   Upcoming sales in major department stores
D   Continuous waves of rippling ecstasy

8   What is your most romantic location for love making?

A   Chest deep in crystal clear waters of Mauritian lagoon
B   Weston-super-Mare
C   Changing room at Emporio Armani
D   Back stage at Def Leppard concert

9   What does oral sex mean to you?

A   Getting a man where you want him
B   Saying 'No'
C   Telephone shopping
D   Listening to a French waiter talk through the specials

**10   What are you most likely to say after
       making love?**

A   What's your name?
B   Let's get down to Mothercare
C   I see your underpants are Calvin Klein
D   That's what I call teamwork!

Mostly As

You have a normal healthy sex drive. You think about it night and day and have a knee-high pile of discarded men's underwear by your bed.

Mostly Bs

Sex for you is as exciting as taking the rubbish out. In fact that's probably how your refer to a night out with your partner.

Mostly Cs

Sex to you is a sublimation of your obsession with shopping. Nothing turns you on faster than a sale sign and for you the sexiest undressing is what you do in a fitting room.

Mostly Ds

You are in some form of community care, probably a weird religious community. You like to express yourself through sex which keeps you busy because of your multiple personalities.

STRESS

❏ Twenty-four hours from ulcer

S tress is to the 1990s what the starched collar was to business in the 1890s; no one likes it, it serves no useful purpose and it's a pain in the neck.

In fact some people love stress. Male executives like to boast about it in the lavatory, comparing how many ulcers they've got, how many marriages they've had and how long their doctors have given them to live. And then the bastards carry on working twenty hour days until they're eighty.

On the other hand it is no longer acceptable to say your job has no stress. Admitting that your job is stress-free implies you sit there like a vegetable all day staring into space. If your job doesn't have stress it's obviously not worth doing or it's some sort of medieval peasant type job like eel watching or stone masonry or advertising.

The best way to avoid stress is to give stress. If you're a boss and you've got too much on your plate, just scrape it onto someone else's plate. Where's the stress in that? If you're not a boss then you can shout and scream and hold your breath till you go blue – and then come out of the stationery cupboard and go back to your desk.

Many stressed business people find it a comfort to have complex toys on their desk which have no real purpose but are good for fiddling

IT'S A STRESS FRACTURE

around with, for example computers. Real executive toys that seriously reduce stress are things like a spanking new BMW 7-series or a second home in Tuscany.

Highly stressed bosses try and pretend they're like chocolates – tough on the outside but with a soft fondant centre. If, during great stress, you've ever bitten your boss, you'll know this is true.

KEY LEARNINGS
- **Stress is life-affirming**
- **It proves you're alive**
- **Until it kills you and then it loses it's effect so why worry?**

Ten tell-tale signs of stress

1 Hair goes grey overnight
2 Total hair loss next night
3 All body hair disappears
4 Thick hair growth in ears
5 Nightmares about work during day at work
6 Continual shaking, spinning and other symptoms reminiscent of Seventies' dancing
7 Bad driving habits: golf handicap increases
8 Staring blankly at computer screen when you don't work with computers
9 Uncontrollable bad language and obscene gestures when presenting to the Board
10 Returning from holiday white (especially if you're black)

PERSONAL CRISES
❏ Unleash the blubbing wimp within you

The best form of entertainment in the office is the personal crisis. This is where someone loses their temper or breaks down or tells a valued business customer to deep fry their genitals. Everyone has these crises. For some it's simmering resentment for thirty years followed by a sudden outbreak of eczema. For others, mostly men, it takes the form of very loud shouting, swearing and storming about the office. Actual physical fights are rare and tend to be between sales people who have forgotten the finer points of negotiation.

During one of these male outbursts, you should strenuously resist the urge to titter. Men who are shouting are expressing all the classic symptoms of insecurity, lack of confidence and possible deficiency in the underpant department. Therefore the last thing they want to see is a load of tittering ninnies hiding behind their computers. This is why they will move rapidly into the 'you're fired' phase, followed twenty-four hours later by the bunches of flowers phase and a month later by the 'early retirement' phase. It has to be said that not all men are like this. A violent outburst from an HR director is as likely as a burst of wit from a finance director.

Female crises in the office tend to take the form of tears and sobbing. When a woman breaks down in tears, every other woman for fifty miles joins in the handkerchief waving and general clearing up. This is due to deep instinctive feelings of sisterly support and, more importantly, a burning desire to get all the dirt and gossip first hand. One of the calming things women say to each other in moments of crises is 'He's not worth it'. This is a deeply held conviction that the male in question does not have the professional accomplishments to justify his large salary.

However distraught they are, women will always grab their handbag before running to the loo in tears. Similarly, men grab their wallets before they rush out of the office to the pub. The number of times men have to do this shows just how sensitive they are underneath.

KEY LEARNINGS
- **Don't store feelings of anger within you**
- **They should be stored in the anger cupboard**
- **If you want to take out your anger, you must sign for it**

SICKIES
❑ Succumb to the power of your duvet

Given the number of people off sick at any one time, it's not surprising that the National Health Service is in crisis. In reality the closest that most people off sick get to the NHS is when they drive past a hospital on their way to the South Coast. That's because people aren't going to take a sickie unless they're well enough to enjoy it.

You can take a maximum of three days off with a sickie before you are required to have a doctor's note, which these days you have to pay for. You would have thought that for a few extra quid you could get yourself excused for a couple of months with some seriously nasty tropical stomach bug that tends to flare up around the time of major events in the racing calendar.

Illnesses that occur during a working day have a range of symptoms which tend to peak in number and intensity around about 8.30 in the morning and then rapidly dwindle to a light, generalised nausea by 9.30, for which the only cure is a rigorous bout of shopping. Of course the best sickie of all is maternity leave as you get months and months off. The only disadvantage is that, in order to make it look convincing, you have to bring up a family for the next twenty years.

If you have to phone in to let the office know you're sick, it's very important that you sound like you have pulled the tubes out of your nose and the oxygen mask off your face just to speak to them for a second before you collapse back into a coma. This can be done in a number of ways, the quickest and most effective being to put cotton wool up both nostrils and then to speak through your face flannel. On no account phone in sick from your mobile phone while driving on the motorway with 'I'm walking on sunshine' playing on the CD.

KEY LEARNINGS
- **If you ever get tired of shopping, try a day in the office**
- **Long weekends start with a slight temperature on Friday morning**
- **'The Black Death' does not look convincing in a forged doctor's note**

Sioned Davies – Queen of the Sickie

Days off	Pathetic excuse
72	Headache (possibly migraine)
56	Some kind of nasty stomach thing
40	Repetitive Strain Injury (from forging doctors' notes)
31	Electrician/plumber/Dynorod
25	Sixteen dental appointments (+ nine dental hygienists)
20	Bus or car engine failure
12	Catworming
8	Miscellaneous
7	Weddings (three her own)
6	Life threatening illness of parent
4	Uncontactable, presumed missing
4	House moves
3	Grandmothers' funerals
2	Convalescence subsequent to bikini area depilation disaster
1	Tights – ladder in

SICK OFFICE SYNDROME
❏ A national contagion

Sick office syndrome is not where two evil little perverts from Accounts discuss what they'd like to do with Sharon Stone on a wet weekend. Instead it refers to offices which make people feel ill. Of course they haven't yet built the office that makes people feel full of the joys of spring, but we're talking about offices that make you feel queasy and nauseous even before you do any work. There are three things that affect your health in the office and they are all TLAs (Three Letter Acronyms).

The first is RSI (Repetitive Strain Injury). This sounds like what you get after one too many repeats of *Dad's Army*. In fact it's occupational hazards like 'paper clip finger' suffered by people who photocopy too much and have fingers that look like minced beef because of the number of staples they have to pull out. Top executives also get RSI. In their case it's called luncher's gut which is the symptom of persistent and repetitive abuse of the expense account.

SAD stands for Seasonal Affective Disorder. This is where you get to the end of February and you feel an overwhelming desire to be on a beach in the Caribbean. Most people have this desire all year round but when you get it in February you get a special TLA to go with it and the chance of a sick note from your psychiatrist. The opposite of SAD is MAD (Midsummer Affective Disorder) where people get a little bit of sun on their head and decide to cavort naked round the office wearing nothing but a strategically positioned internal memo.

By far and away the most dangerous affliction in the office is the CLM (Career Limiting Move). This is where you do something so badly misjudged that your career, pay packet and mental health are all abruptly terminated. An example of this would be if you made a formal complaint about sick office syndrome to the Managing Director when you worked in the corporate headquarters of BUPA.

KEY LEARNINGS
- **Sick leave shortens your working life**
- **No one's ever too weak to pick up a pay packet**
- **Headaches are often contagious during major sporting events**

MASSAGE
❏ Hands-on management

Companies who have downsized so completely that they only have three people left to do the work have suddenly realised that they better be nice to those remaining otherwise they're going to be in deep dog parp business-wise. That's why employees are now offered marvellous comforting things that they wouldn't dream of indulging in at home.

For example, a new benefit is the at-your-desk massage. This is usually a light finger-tip massage to relieve stress in the shoulders, so there's no point sitting stark naked at your desk, clutching a bottle of baby oil and grinning like an idiot. At companies where computers are used intensively, staff are being offered free eye tests, which sounds good but usually amounts to 'Can you see your computer? Yes, well get on with it.'

Mental health is also catered for by a rash of 'executive coaches'. These are weirdy-beardy types who sit in your office and listen to you talk about the problems of shrinking return on assets and then tell you that if you unblock your energy channels in your lower chakras then everything will be tickety-boo. They then recommend a further course of treatment that will significantly enhance your cash flow, mostly in the direction of their wallet.

Yoga in the office is another hot new thing, especially the Lotus Notes position. This is where you work on your computer with one leg wrapped around the back of your neck, preferably your own leg. In yoga there is also a special 'wind releasing' position which reduces digestive stress. This involves lying on your back and clutching your knees to your chest. Meetings in the advertising industry often consist solely of executives hunched for an hour or two in the wind releasing position.

KEY LEARNINGS
- **Never, ever relax completely at work**
- **Lunch time aerobics are no excuse for leotards in team meetings**
- **Your boss won't be wanting a stress relieving massage from you when they are giving you the mother of all bollockings**

BUSINESS DRINKING
❑ Living with your liver

Alcohol and business don't mix. Which is why if you like a drink you really shouldn't bother with work. Excessive drinking at work makes you feel sociable, light-headed and confident that you can do anything. In other words it makes you feel like you work in marketing.

The day after, when you feel like the whole world is a grim, head-crushing torture chamber, it makes you feel like you work in the IT department.

IF YOU WANT TO IMPRESS AT A BUSINESS LUNCH DON'T ORDER SPAGHETTI

Drinking at lunch time is a great pleasure not only for those who do it, but also for those who work for those who do it. That's because afternoons become the time when you can get your expenses signed, your four-week holiday approved and your salary doubled just by lifting your boss's head off their desk, smiling sweetly and putting the appropriate form in front of their nose. Of course when we're talking about lunch time drinking, we don't mean half a lager shandy – we mean drinking so much you have to get a taxi back to the office from the pub across the street.

Certain industries drink more heavily than others. The computer industry is virtually teetotal because computers can't yet decipher drunken commands that read like the pet name of the Polish foreign minister. In industries such as PR where clarity of thinking is a professional disadvantage, drinking is mandatory until the desired level of mindless bonhomie is achieved. The heaviest drinkers of all are operators of heavy machinery who drink to forget the fact that they are forbidden to use anti-histamines because of possible drowsiness.

Saddest of all are the boozy old lags who sit around for hours drinking themselves senseless and broadcasting their personal inadequacies in a loud voice. Yet somehow these board meetings always seem to sober up at the critical moment and vote themselves wallet-bending share options.

KEY LEARNINGS
- **Think before you drink before you drive (normal people)**
- **Drive before you drink before you think (sales people)**
- **Drink before you think before you drive (MD on golfing weekend)**

LUNCHING

❏ The asparagus spear as business weapon

The idea of a free lunch is so powerful that a whole industry has grown up around it. This industry is called corporate hospitality and it's based on the fact that people who wouldn't think of meeting you for an ordinary meeting will happily meet you for lunch, especially if it's served in a directors' box before a rugby international at Twickenham.

No act of corporate hospitality is complete without everyone getting a big golfing umbrella with a logo printed on it. These are very useful at outdoor events because God disapproves of corporate hospitality and tends to rain on it. Clients can easily tell how big their budgets are by the number of suppliers' umbrellas clogging up their hall at home.

Corporate hospitality is mostly done by suppliers for their clients and the idea is to get them so drunk that the years of appalling, overpriced service are wiped from their memory. It helps matters if you take them to a sporting event redolent of British success, like women's hockey or coxless pairs.

There is of course a subtle line where corporate hospitality becomes downright bribery. This line is so subtle that most people from marketing never notice it, especially when they've just finished their second bottle of champagne and they've started mooning to the crowd from a box at Anfield. Naturally, finance departments rigorously disapprove of all freebies as for them giving out a biro with the company name on is tantamount to grand larceny.

In the end it's all about style. Do clients give their business to suppliers who fly them to Paris for the races or to suppliers who are working so hard on their behalf that their corporate entertainment amounts to no more than a couple of luncheon vouchers stapled to their invoice? Clients with their heads screwed on will go to Paris with the first company and give their business to the second.

I'VE HAD MY WORKING LUNCH
NOW I'M HAVING MY WORKING NAP

KEY LEARNINGS

- **All work and no play makes Jack unlikely to get the big contract**
- **Wads of cash in brown envelopes are the most sincere form of hospitality**
- **Never take a client you hope to impress to see Wales play football**

~ CHAPTER 4 ~

STATIONERY, HANDBAGS AND FIRST AID KITS

Never commit to paper, to memory or to women with nervous tics.
Pieter Bamfjord ~ Twentieth-century Norwegian cynic and troll breeder

STATIONERY
❑ Cupboard love

Stationery cupboards are the sweet shops of office life. They're a sort of colourful pick and mix of lots of nice little things that you don't really need but you nevertheless keep helping yourself to, until your desk looks like a small branch of WH Smith's.

Hardback notebooks are top on the list of removables. You use the first page and then lose interest on the second because the paper isn't quite so squeaky clean. Also available are huge hole punchers that could perforate a rhino's scrotum. It's only when you've punched holes through every document within five yards of your desk that you realise the hole spacing is only compatible with filing systems in old Soviet Bloc countries.

Another hot item in the stationery cupboard is highlighter pens. These highlight the useful and important parts of documents and prove that ninety per cent of most documents are neither. 'Things to do' pads go like hot cakes because they give the impression that you're getting organised. Stationery is in fact a work substitute and you'll notice that the first three things you write on your 'Things to do' pad are '1. Highlight documents. 2. Punch holes in documents. 3. Staple documents.'

So much is stolen from stationery cupboards that they have to be protected behind signs which say 'High Voltage. Danger of Death'. Sadly these signs are also stolen and stuck on the desk of volatile managers as a bit of a joke.

There is a certain virgin sweetness about stationery items which is evidenced by people's resistance to reusing old lever arch files marked 'Bought Ledger 1974'. Inevitably, some office workers develop quite a fetish for stationery. It's not unheard of for someone working late to pop into the stationery cupboard and find the Sales Director sitting inside, stark naked, covered head to foot in Post-it notes.

KEY LEARNINGS
- **No one has ever come out of a stationery cupboard empty-handed**
- **Except in Saudi Arabia**
- **Where you can steal from the stationery cupboard a maximum of twice**

Ten items of stationery and what they say about your sexuality

1	Index cards	*Hugely promiscuous*
2	Tippex	*Regret past mistakes*
3	Sellotape	*Secret desire for bondage*
4	Photocopy toner	*Masochist*
5	Hole puncher	*Dominant*
6	Highlighter	*Easily excited*
7	Flip charts	*Show off*
8	Rubber bands	*Sexual deviant*
9	Notebook	*Voyeur*
10	Sasco Year Planner	*Optimistic*

CHAPTER 4

SELLOTAPE
❏ Sticking with it

There are two types of Sellotape users: those who mark the end of the tape with a little piece of paper or fold the end over nice and neatly and then feel pretty smug about it. Then there are the rest of us who pick up the roll, hold it three inches in front of our face and turn it round an average of eighteen times looking for the end. When we find it, we rip it into three little threads none of which ever amounts to a proper width of tape.

It's a sad fact about Sellotape that the average person uses 32 feet a year which amounts to about half a large roll. For the metric minded, that's half a large metric roll. The same average person takes at least six rolls a year from the stationery cupboard. That's about 800 per cent more than they need. So where does it all go? Who knows, but it's high time there was a Blue Peter appeal to turn all those unused rolls into a new high-speed rail link to the Channel Tunnel.

One of the things about Sellotape is that, unlike babies, it gets stickier as it gets older. When you start work you put up posters like 'You don't have to be mad to work here but it helps', which you then have to rip down pretty smartish when you're promoted to Staff Welfare Manager. In the meantime the Sellotape has acquired the sticking power of an anally retentive barnacle and you're likely to pull down a hundredweight of plaster and the best part of your office.

Sellotape is only one of a large family of sticky tapes that includes the famous Gaffer tape. This is a sort of macho black tape which rock group roadies use to stick bundles of wires together. A popular game amongst roadies is to stick gaffer tape to their mates' chests while they are in a drug-induced coma and then watch them try to rip it off when they wake up. The resulting noise was one of the formative influences in heavy metal music.

KEY LEARNINGS
- **The end is the beginning (T.S. Eliot)**
- **The stickiest tape is red tape**
- **Sellotape can be a useful tool for male bonding**

BRIEFCASES
❏ Getting a handle on them

In the commercial world it is the height of bad taste to have anything business related in your briefcase. Briefcases are for taking the contents of the stationery cupboard home with you at the end of the day. Only photocopier repairmen have their work in their briefcases – fifteen different screwdrivers, a copy of the *Sun* and a list of exotic, faraway locations from where the vital missing part will have to be shipped in a couple of months' time.

When it comes to briefcases, size is important and, amazingly, smaller is better. Really top executives have briefcases so slim that sandwiches will only fit in if they are evenly spread Marmite on thin-sliced Mother's Pride. A briefcase larger than A2 constitutes an art bag and you run the risk of being mistaken for an advertising executive which is the business equivalent of a personal hygiene problem.

Some briefcases have concertina sections which expand to hold pyjamas, computers and overhead projectors. Remember to clear this out when you come back from trips abroad. Otherwise you'll open your case up for a key presentation and your wife's nightie will billow out onto the boardroom table. Alternatively don't take the nightie on business trips.

Briefcases with combination locks can resist the most determined attempts to get in them especially by the people who own them. When you're in airport arrivals being hassled by a Colombian customs officer, it's comforting to know that the likelihood of you getting your combination right under pressure is the same as winning the National Lottery two weeks running.

NEVER CHANGE YOUR BRIEFCASE COMBINATION BEFORE A CRUCIAL MEETING

Business generally is more relaxed now and some people go to work with their papers in a satchel or knapsack or bin liner. Be warned that some areas of business are less relaxed than others and if you're a top merchant banker you won't get very far if you roll up to meetings with your papers in a *Jurassic Park* lunchbox.

KEY LEARNINGS

- **A man's briefs should never be larger than his briefcase**
- **A Concorde luggage tag has a life expectancy equal to three briefcases**
- **Don't carry a monogrammed briefcase if your name is Terry Ian Trent**

Ten things Corporate Raiders don't have in their briefcases

1   *Viz*
2   Teachings of Jesus
3   Turkish in three months
4   Pressed flowers
5   Home made fudge
6   Bus timetable
7   'The Flowers of Gentleness' poetry collection
8   Leotard
9   Small soft toy
10   Smelling salts

THE BIRO
❏ Something to chew on

Biros are like Japanese cars. They're cheap, they start first time and they come in many colours. Of course Japanese cars don't have the little unexplained hole in the side but then as we know our Japanese friends are obsessed with quality. The most common biro is the Bic biro, named after its inventor Hugo Tampon, who for understandable reasons changed his name to Hugo Bic.

Twenty-six million biros are produced annually in Britain, of which ninety-five per cent are used and then thrown away. The other five per cent go to biro heaven in the top pockets of train spotters and distribution managers in warehouses. In the subtle hierarchies that rule the world of train spotting, preference on the platform is often given to those with the rare and much prized green biro.

A great mystery is what happens to the tops of biros, the little plastic things that look like a Fifties' representation of a space ship. Detailed research, were someone dull enough to do it, would probably show that most biro tops are permanently separated from their pens within the first thirty minutes of use. These tops have been specially designed not to be useful for any other function in the world except one, and that is executive nipple substitute. To the highly stressed, a biro is a complete meal. First you bend back the clip bit from the top and then bite it off. Then you mangle the top between your teeth, suck out the little stopper from the top of the pen, and crunch away at the pen itself. Real addicts chew down the inside plastic bit and wash it down with a mouthful of ink.

Very occasionally a biro will dry up on you even though you can clearly see that most of the ink is still in it. This generally happens when you're signing a multi-million pound deal or a major peace treaty. Remember, it's no good scrubbing away at the paper with heavy-handed loop the loops, ticks and cross hatching. It'll ruin the treaty and it won't work. Simply breathe deeply, accept the fact that if it doesn't restart after a couple of good strokes it's dead, and consign it and world peace to the dustbin.

KEY LEARNINGS
- **Japanese obsession with quality**
- **Biros are valuable fibre supplement**
- **Fragile nature of world peace**

Biro hoarders – the big top five

Person	Position	Total in pocket
Alfred 'Voidoid' Smedley	Superintendent Lavatories (Royal Parks)	17
Jimmy 'the Bic' Hinds	Assistant Track (sidings) Admin Officer, Network SE	12
Ernie 'Ink Stain' Carmichael	National Philately Bureau (1st day covers), Hackney	11
Henty 'Popperpoint' O'Rourke	Assistant Archivist, BNFL (Lytham St. Anne's)	10
Sir Gus Nodwell	Chief Executive Officer, British Valves	6

CALCULATORS
❏ Knowing the hot buttons

Pocket calculators are everywhere these days. In fact the only place you'll never find one is in someone's pocket. Calculators are now so cheap that you can add them to anything with virtually no extra cost which is why you get things like ironing boards with built-in calculator to work out your exact ironing time per underpant.

Generally the bigger the calculator the more insignificant the person. Truly piddling people have calculators with buttons big enough for a pig's trotter, a fat addition sign that you can operate with the side of your palm and a little roll of paper that churns out all those vital petty cash figures. If you own one of these, or more than three calculators in total, you are well equipped to work out just how sad you really are as a percentage of total sadness.

If you paid more than £10 for your calculator it is probably 'scientific' with more computing power than the whole of Albania. Nevertheless, it's worth paying the extra money because you never know when you're going to need to work out the fractal coefficient of the hypotenuse of xy. No one has ever used all the buttons on a scientific calculator probably because about half don't actually mean anything and are just there to impress people who failed maths O level.

All the rage now are solar-powered calculators. In Britain these work for about three days a year, just long enough to let you work out the average annual rainfall. The latest smart calculators interact with you. For example the baker's calculator always throws in a couple extra just to be nice while the Financial Director's calculator gives you your total and then a little message saying, 'That doesn't look good, does it Jeremy'. In the advertising industry totals are automatically doubled with the message, 'They'll never notice'.

IF THIS IS FANTASY FOOTBALL WE'RE LAUGHING. IF IT'S THE SALES FIGURES WE'RE NOT

KEY LEARNINGS
- Calculators don't actually know how to do percentages
- Smart calculators turn themselves on three days before you get paid
- Management consultants give their clients shock-proof calculators for Christmas

BUSINESS CARDS
❑ Your proof that you exist in business life

Business cards are the driving licenses of the business world without which you don't really exist. Ninety-nine per cent of these cards are in one of two places; the top drawer of the desk of the person who owns them or the bin of the person who just received one.

The first thing anyone looks at on the card is your title which will be either Executive, Manager, or Director. In a big meeting the cool thing to do is to arrange the cards you've been given in rank order in front of you and then address all your comments to the Executive, who will be the most junior person there. If you have more than three words in your job title then this is a sure-fire indication that you have a Mickey Mouse job. Take for example, Executive Production Manager or Client Services Director or Deputy Prime Minister. Much better to have just one unequivocal word on your card like Chairman, Owner, Founder or God.

Recently there has been a bit of a fad for putting something on the back of your business card. This is a bit of a swizz because this space is specifically designed for noting people's home numbers or designing a new jet engine. Yet you'll see wide boys of all descriptions with Japanese or Arabic translations on the backs of their cards. This is a bit unnecessary when they sell double glazing door to door. If they could actually read Japanese they would know that the text actually reads, 'Beware round-eye wide boy with dodgy double glazing. Say you are in conservation area.'

The weediest, saddest thing you can do in business is give someone a card so old it has a phone number without the extra one followed by a telex number, and then say 'we're just having some new ones printed'. Let's face it, you're going out of business, so don't expect them to waste one of their new cards with e-mail address and extra one in the phone number on you.

KEY LEARNINGS
- **Non-standard size business cards have the shelf life of bio-yoghurt**
- **Big business deals aren't secured by handing out your card on busy street corners**
- **If you don't like someone, put a stamp on their card and pop it in the post**

PHOTOCOPIERS
❏ The new business toner

The difference between your standard office photocopier and the Women's Institute stall at the village fete is that the photocopier gives you jams every day of the year. Photocopiers have three natural states: On, Off and Out of Order. The third state is the photocopier's natural resting place between the first two states. If photocopiers were cars you would be able to drive three miles before your engine blew up and those three miles would normally be on the way to hospital for a life-saving operation.

There are now some very fancy high-tech photocopiers on the market which can give you a hundred sorted and collated documents within a minute. Sadly, the technology is so exciting that you often end up with a hundred sorted and collated blank pieces of paper because you put the original in upside down.

There is an old and respected tradition amongst male office workers that during the office party the more excitable among them will decide that it's time to photocopy their genitals. At this stage it's always interesting to note who pushes the enlarge button before copying. If you are going to take part in this ritual it's important that you do it before you are too drunk as you might end up using the shredder by mistake.

There are two messages that your average secretary dreads. One is 'Can you work late, Judith?' The other is 'Add Toner'. Photocopier toner is specially developed to run out only on the days when you are wearing your spanking new cream silk blouse. When you have finished ever so carefully changing the toner your silk blouse will look like a Welsh miner's donkey jacket. This fact often leads people to wonder why photocopier repairmen always turn up in natty suits. The answer is that all they ever do is lift the lid, suck their teeth and tell you that they will need to order a part that costs more than your annual salary and will be delivered shortly before you retire.

KEY LEARNINGS
- In evolutionary terms the photocopier is the direct descendant of the mangle
- Prolonged exposure to photocopiers causes socks to turn white
- 'Can I have a copy' is the corporate equivalent of, 'It's nice to see you'.

Ten songs dedicated to the photocopier

1 Pump up the jam
2 When a man loves a Hewlett Packard
3 Something's got a hold of my document
4 Una Minolta Blanca
5 You ain't seen nothin' yet (and you're not likely to)
6 Simply the worst (Tina Toner)
7 Rip it up (and start again)
8 Torn between two rollers
9 Que Feeder Espana
10 Xeroxanne

FIRST AID KITS
❏ Dealing with personal injury claims

The office First Aid kit is like the G spot. Everyone knows it's there, but no one can quite put their hands on it. Like the G Spot, finding the First Aid kit can prove to be a disappointment. For some reason they all seem to comprise seven large triangular bandages. These would be handy if a light plane crash landed in the office but otherwise they're completely useless. Who's ever going to say, 'I've dislocated my collar bone. Don't worry about the ambulance, just pass me one of those triangular bandages and I'll press on with this report'? No one.

All offices are supposed to have a trained First Aider. This tends to be the office leper with the thermonuclear halitosis. Unfortunately, people would sooner volunteer for open heart surgery from the maintenance man than mouth-to-mouth with him. A much more useful job for the office First Aider would be to go round to the homes of people who were off sick and see if they were as ill as they sounded on the telephone.

Many First Aid kits come with helpful emergency guidelines such as what to do in the event of a tidal wave or an all-out chemical and biological attack. What they don't do is give hints on the real office emergencies such as a broken fingernail or a boss with post-lunch snappiness. It's probably just as well as the solution would probably involve several large triangular bandages.

Real First Aid kits should be kept in the office fridge and should consist of a number of ice cold gin and tonics. If you insist on having a First Aid tin these should packed with headache pills, powerful anti-depressants and disposable nappies for use in annual appraisals. Of course what's in a First Aid kit is largely academic, because when it comes to locating it in an emergency, you've got more chance of finding the Holy Grail.

KEY LEARNINGS
- **UK offices have more bandages than were used in the entire Crimean war**
- **On average a woman has 6.8 Nurofen in her handbag**
- **Back problems generally mean workers who don't come back**

HANDBAGS
❑ What they say about you and how to shut them up

A working woman's handbag is an office, washroom, databank, first aid centre, counselling department, long-term warehouse, travelling suitcase and financial department all rolled into one, chic little off-the-shoulder number.

Women's handbags also have a separate mini handbag in them which is like a lunar module that goes out from the main mother handbag on smaller voyages. There is also a substantial business compartment in women's handbags which will generally hold the personal organiser, itself the size and weight of a full desk drawer. Small photocopiers have been known to fit comfortably in larger handbags.

There is a dark inner pocket in most handbags which harbours women's mystical personal things, connected with strange and hushed druidical rites that seem to come round on a monthly basis. How ever deeply these strange personal things are packed into the handbag they always pop out and land in the middle of the desk when the personal organiser is pulled out at the start of an important meeting.

Women are very conscious of bag snatching especially when on foreign trips and sensibly clasp their bags with both hands firmly against the body with the strap wound twice round their body and through their legs much like a parachute harness. Men should beware of touching or interfering with a woman's handbag in any way as this is tantamount to sexual harassment.

At the bottom of every woman's handbag is the small anvil which is the thing that shatters your pelvis when you come into contact with it in a lift or crowded train. The weight of the average women's handbag is 60 kilograms, slightly below what the SAS are required to carry on long night marches.

Every woman has something odd in her handbag that, should she suddenly be buried by an erupting volcano, would give archaeologists a thousand years from now cause for endless speculation and debate. These items include things such as primus stoves, hacksaw blades, valances, hockey balls, red Y-fronts and petrol caps.

KEY LEARNINGS
- You can get the contents of the British Museum into five handbags
- With space left for a box of tissues
- When a handbag is emptied completely it dies

~ CHAPTER 5 ~

MEETINGS, TEAMWORK AND CUSTOMERS

There is no 'I' in 'team'. But there is in 'after dinner mint'.

Hindenberg Johnson ~ Twentieth-century Jamaican surrealist and Rotarian

◆

MEETINGS
❏ What are they for exactly?

Half of every working day is spent in meetings, half of which are not worth having, and of those that are, half the time is wasted. Which means that nearly one third of business life is spent in small rooms with people you don't like, doing things that don't matter. The only reason people have so many meetings is that they're the one time you can get away from your work, your phone and your customers.

People say that the secret of a good meeting is preparation. But if people really prepared for meetings, the first thing they would realise is that most are completely unnecessary. In fact a tightly run meeting is one of the most frightening things in office life. These are meetings before which you have to prepare, in which you have to work and after which you have to take actions. Fortunately, these meetings are as rare as a sense of adventure in the finance department. One of these meetings in January is generally sufficient to give a medium-sized company enough momentum for the whole year.

There is no such thing as an interesting meeting. That's why no one ever comes out of a meeting saying 'Wow that was a fantastic meeting, let's have another one now instead of going home.' You can judge how tedious meeting are by the doodles they generate. Anything that looks like the product of a spider on acid means you're in the worst of all meetings, the status meeting. These are so-called because everyone tries to prove their status by talking loudly about their own achievements.

Time in meetings is always different from real time. A quick ten-minute catch-up can fill a whole morning. One of the reasons for this is that work in meetings doesn't actually start until someone says, 'I've got a meeting to go to'.

KEY LEARNINGS
- A cancelled meeting is the sweetest thing in office life
- Legally a sales meeting with more than eight people constitutes 'riotous assembly'
- When accountants meet, somewhere a little bird stops singing

---

Ten meetings that are a total and utter waste of time

1 Appraisals
2 Teambuilding
3 Meetings with IT people
4 Planning meetings
5 Finance meetings
6 Marketing meetings
7 Sales meetings
8 Meetings with Personnel Department
9 Meetings with agencies or consultancies
10 Meetings with any form of management – senior, middle or junior

MORE MEETINGS
❏ Won't you stay just a little bit longer

WHAT DID YOU DO IN THE OFFICE TODAY DAD?

I'VE NO IDEA

Meetings are like church services. Once you're in one you can't stand up, shout that it's all rubbish and then walk out. Of course you can try it but then you run the risk of being excommunicated or, if things turn nasty, being burnt at the stake. And it's not much better if you walk out of church.

When you go on a week's holiday you miss on average ten meetings, but curiously no one misses you. That's because meetings have a life of their own regardless of the people in them. The moral of this is that whenever someone asks you to be in a meeting say that although nothing would give you more pleasure than being bored rigid by them for three hours, sadly you are going to be on holiday. For a week after, carry a suitcase rather than a briefcase round the office in case someone spots you walking past a meeting you are supposed to be in.

Meetings are also a lot like car heaters in the Austin Allegro – they just recycle hot air until you get a headache and have to open the window. Like the Austin Allegro itself, having a meeting must have seemed like a good idea to someone at sometime, but when it actually happens everyone realises that it's a total waste of time and money, and won't get you anywhere without a great deal of pain, personal misery, wrong turnings, smoke and foul language.

Most meetings are spent either talking about problems arising from work that hasn't been done or talking about work that needs to be done to tackle problems. There are so many of these meetings that there is very little time to do any work or solve problems, which means only one thing – more meetings.

KEY LEARNINGS
- **Meetings move at the pace of the slowest mind**
- **If your meeting is still going after six hours, shoot someone**
- **If that doesn't help, set fire to yourself in protest**

BREAKFAST MEETINGS
❑ Bring home the bacon

Power breakfasts are like power lunches except no one's really awake. If your boss insists on having breakfast meetings, creep through the door in your dressing gown and sit huddled in your Ryan Giggs duvet. Every time they try to get the meeting underway start shaving or doing your make-up (or both) and say 'Is this going to take long, I've got to get ready for work?'

One of the problems with business breakfasts is that you can never eat what you normally have for breakfast. No one's going to be impressed at a top level breakfast meeting if you're tucking into a bowl full of Kellogg's Coco Pops. Instead you have to eat things like grapefruit and croissants that only religious zealots and French people would touch.

The only tolerable business breakfast is the one you have on the train. If you have a meeting in another city you can have a big breakfast on your way up, cancel your meeting, and then have a big lunch on the way back. Railway companies make more money from their breakfasts than they do on any of their train services. In fact the sausage alone is a greater source of revenue than the Fort William sleeper.

One of the nastiest sights in the business world is middle-aged secretaries in cardigans eating sad bowls of muesli at the beginning of the day. They are under the pathetic illusion that this will make them healthy and vibrant even though they always have to follow up the muesli with a fistful of pills for high blood pressure, fallen arches, weak gonads and a whole range of other ailments.

Power breakfasts are supposed to give the impression that you've already been to the gym and that you're on top form at six in the morning. It's some sort of dreadful macho thing and next time some braying yuppie suggests it try replying, 'No, but I can squeeze you in at three thirty this afternoon for a power cup of tea and a couple of power Jammy Dodgers.'

KEY LEARNINGS
- Only agree to business breakfasts if they're in bed
- No one would have breakfast meetings if kippers were served
- Security guards will happily take your place at breakfast meetings for a small consideration

STARTING WORK
❑ Delaying the inevitable

S tarting work is a very difficult period in life, and one which we have to go through every morning of the week. However, just because you've arrived at the office, doesn't mean you have to plunge straight into work. The first essential requirement is coffee. Theoretically work can start without coffee in the same way that theoretically a car can start without petrol. Carbohydrates are also important and a couple of slices of toast and jam will markedly improve your efficiency throughout the day.

The next step is reading the mail. It doesn't matter who it's addressed to, as long as it's read. We work in the information age which means reading the papers in the morning is a vital piece of information gathering. Naturally horoscopes need to be consulted. If you're going to make things happen in the office, there's no point in fighting against vast cosmic forces. The *Financial Times* is the only paper you can get away with reading in front of your boss, unless you work in advertising where even the *Beano* will mark you out as a dangerous intellectual.

Teamwork is never more vital than at the beginning of the day. This means checking how the rest of the team slept last night, who they slept with and whether they had to chew their arm off to get away. If you're really going to clear the decks for action, make sure any outstanding gossip is dealt with at the beginning of the day. This also leaves the rest of the day clear for any late-breaking gossip.

Finally you should look at the work in hand and see whether, in the interests of the environment, energy could be saved by ignoring it. If not, check to see if you have a headache. It's amazing how you can pick up the beginnings of one if you concentrate hard enough. This might then warrant a day off, or at the very least a stroll to the pub for some fresh air.

KEY LEARNINGS
- **Why put off today something that can be put off tomorrow**
- **Fools rush in where wise men delegate**
- **A stitch in time will have to be unpicked at the last moment**

WORKING LATE
❑ Look at it as a very early start

Anyone who finds themselves working late on a regular basis is on a steep downward spiral on a coconut mat marked stress. Sadly, it's their own fault because when they were asked in their interview if they were prepared to work long, unsociable hours, they didn't reply, 'No, I prefer to work short, sociable ones, thank you.'

Of course definitions of what late working means vary. If you work nine to five and you find yourself still in the building at 5.35 then that's a pretty late night. If on the other hand you run your own business and you leave the office before last orders then that amounts to a half day.

In big offices the definition of late working is if you know the names of the cleaner's children and the name of the security guard's unfortunate skin condition. You also know you're working too late too often if the first time your children are old enough to stay up late enough to welcome you home is shortly before they leave for college.

Nevertheless working late does have its advantages. Obviously the first one is that you can get more work done in three hours than you can in three normal working days because you're not continually distracted by the personal phone calls you're making all the time. It also gives you a golden opportunity to rifle through other people's personal papers and generally get yourself up to speed on the office dirt. Generally it's while you're casually flicking through the Managing Director's in-tray that you discover the one other person who habitually works late happens to be the Managing Director.

In advertising agencies people often have to work late because lunching takes up so much of the day. Working late in advertising means drinking solidly all night and then pulling something out of the waste bin at four in the morning which you present the next day as the mould-breaking creative concept.

KEY LEARNINGS
- **You know you're working late when you start to feel sorry for yourself**
- **You know you're working really late when you eat a pizza with anchovies**
- **You know you're working incredibly late when you dig out all the little anchovies you put in the bin earlier and eat them**

HIGH PERFORMANCE TEAMS
❏ Why we don't have them in sport or business

'Teambuilding' brings together a group of people who don't work well together in the office, takes them to somewhere in the country and then puts them through a series of mental and physical exercises to prove they don't work together out of the office either. There's nothing quite so repellent as seeing your boss turn up to a teambuilding event in casual clothing. He will be wearing jeans that look as if they were standard issue in the Greek Navy at the turn of the century, a chunky woollen sweater knitted by someone in the advanced stages of Alzheimer's, and plimsolls.

During exercises like river crossings someone will need to take charge. If you want to get across the river quickly and without getting wet, let a secretary organise it. Sadly this is the exact time when your boss will want to prove they're the boss by organising a crossing that involves recreating conditions in the office, i.e. everyone standing up to their neck in freezing water while the boss flaps around on the bank attempting to make big strategic decisions. It's generally at this point when someone in sales, who already has a job offer with another company, accidentally lets a rope slip that lowers the boss headfirst into a deep pool of freezing water.

Of course all the tensions of the day will soon be forgotten in the bar where the boss will show off his ability to down a small glass of sweet sherry in six or seven sips. Suitably plastered they will then do something extremely hip like putting Shirley Bassey on the juke box and then start snapping their fingers, which makes everybody else jump up because they think they've forgotten to do something.

The worst part of teambuilding are so-called trust exercises where you're suddenly expected to trust someone who has done everything in their power to thwart your career for the last ten years. These trust exercises involve falling backward with your eyes closed to be caught by your colleagues. If you close your eyes, fall backwards and then open your eyes in an intensive care unit, you can be pretty sure that the team building has been successful but that you're not in the team.

KEY LEARNINGS
- **Mutiny is a fantastic bonding exercise**
- **Live ammunition does wonders for teambuilding exercises**
- **Human sacrifice livens up evening entertainment no end**

DOWNSIZING
❏ Teambuilding in reverse

Firing people is like being in a firing squad. Obviously it's very traumatic pulling the trigger but not quite as traumatic as being shot. Most managers try and make the firing process easier for themselves by pretending that it has nothing to do with them and saying things like: 'It's been decided that you'll be going', 'It looks as if you'll be leaving', or 'Apparently, you're off'.

It would be much more helpful if they told you the real reason you were being fired: 'We've sacking you as Personnel Director, Victor, because you hate people, because your personal hygiene is an environmental catastrophe and because your name is deeply unfashionable.'

Voluntary redundancy is where they offer you lots of money to sack yourself. If they had paid you that kind of money in the first place, they might have got some decent work out of you. Anyway, it's always a nice lesson for MDs who think they're running the world's happiest ship, when every single person in the company applies for voluntary redundancy and queues up for hours to get their application form in first.

Executives complain that the two most stressful things in the office are office politics and firing people. If they combined the two their life would be a lot easier: 'I didn't agree with your proposal, Ralph.' 'Well tough, you're fired.'

Executives wouldn't find sacking people so stressful if they had a bit of fun while doing it. They could blow up your P45 to poster size and put it in reception or throw a surprise leaving party for you with coloured 'You're history, Mr Parsons' balloons.

At least sacking isn't as stressful as taking people on. When you sack someone awful they disappear, but when you take on someone awful you have to live with your mistake grinning at you across the office for years. Until you sack them.

I'VE DOWNSIZED MY LIBRARY

KEY LEARNINGS
- **You won't get far called Victor**
- **Get a first name Mr Parsons**
- **Don't mess with Ralph**

INTERNAL COMMUNICATIONS
❏ Uncorking the power of gossip

A lot of companies talk earnestly about how important internal communications are. By internal communication they mean the process by which the bosses tell everyone what is happening followed by a feedback stage where everyone can tell the bosses what they think of what is happening. Then there is a third phase when the bosses sack everybody involved in the feedback process.

Of course every company in the world has an unrivalled internal communication system. This is called gossip. It takes a multinational company five years and lot of pointy headed consultants trailing huge invoices to communicate a new vision to everyone in the company. But if the chairman was to catch his fixed assets in the shredder it would get round every office in the company before you can say, 'Let's keep this quiet shall we'.

Gossip is a highly technical and complex form of communication. For example messages are rigidly prioritised. Personal sexual revelations always take absolute priority over any business message. Of course the hottest news would combine the two, along the lines of 'Anita slept with every single candidate for the IT manager's job, and they've all got second interviews next week.'

Gossip happens all the time in offices and often disguises itself under many different aliases such as 'appraisals' or 'datamergers' or 'top level strategic planning'. E mail is a bit like gossip but will never really replace good face to face bitching. That's because it's almost impossible to imply or insinuate something when you have to type it and when there's also an off chance that you might mistakenly send it to the company newspaper.

ONLY ANOTHER THREE DAYS BEFORE WE GET THE COMPANY NEWSLETTER!

KEY LEARNINGS

- **Gossip is anything likely to be true in the sauciest of all possible worlds**
- **The proof of good gossip is that the first reaction is, 'No!'**
- **HR Departments have all the gossip but none of the naughty bits**

Good internal communications – the five I's

Information   The least possible, to the wrong people, at the last moment, in the wrong way.

Involvement   Make people feel they're actively participating in their last three days with the company

Integration   Message should be consistent with advertising i.e. shallow, patronising and forgettable.

Interaction   Ask what people think and then hold it against them at industrial tribunal

Informality   Using office gossip to spread vicious rumour about downsizing

INNOVATION
❏ Unearth its time-honoured traditions

Innovate or die is the new rallying cry of industry. Well, it's the rallying cry of those parts that aren't dead. For those parts that are still alive, innovation is everything. In Britain more creative thought has been given to improving airline food than to managing the whole economy, which explains why so many people fly British Airways when emigrating. Of course there's nothing new about innovation. We've been innovating since the Stone Age, which largely explains why we're no longer in it.

In order to generate mould-breaking innovations most companies employ the hugely creative idea of a suggestions box. These are then opened at the end of the month and the old Crunchie wrapper is taken out and examined. Yet stories still circulate of how staff suggestions have saved companies millions of pounds – by taking the little cardboard tray out of the bottom of the Bounty Bar or by putting sandpaper on just one side of Swan Vesta matches or by shutting down the whole of British Rail.

Companies even brag about the levels of participation in their company suggestion schemes. The Chairman of Land Rover boasts that he receives more suggestions than any other company in Europe. What he doesn't say is that they're all exactly the same suggestion and no, he won't go until he's good and ready.

Ideas are actually ten a penny in this country. The good ones we give to the Japanese to prop up their ailing economy and the bad ones we keep for ourselves and make into sitcoms. We actually have industries dedicated to creativity. For example our accountancy firms are internationally recognised for their creative accounting. People who think they're creative work in the advertising industry where creativity is measured by how far you can throw your felt-tip pen at the height of your creative tantrum.

KEY LEARNINGS
- **Creativity is a good idea**
- **Innovation is making a good idea happen**
- **Receivership is proof that it wasn't such a good idea after all**

Ten products waiting to be invented

1   Anti-depressant muesli
2   Underwired wonder Y-fronts
3   Sensitive condoms
4   Mango Champagne
5   Beard waxing for men
6   High performance golf cart
7   Geordie speech recognition programme
8   Reading glasses tracker
9   Aphrodisiac steamed treacle pudding
10 Environmentally friendly baked bean

CUSTOMER SERVICE

❏ Learn the secrets and then screw the bastards

All companies swear blind they are customer driven which is a clever way of saying something rather stupid. Let's face it, if you haven't got any customers you haven't got a business. If companies really listened to their customers how come we had to wait so long for the Wonderbra.

In the early Eighties, when you could make money just by sticking your hand out of the window, companies used to have this ridiculous phrase, 'The Customer is King'. Anybody who is a customer of a high street bank or clothes shop will know that the best you ever feel is about a Seven of Clubs.

The other phrase companies use is, 'Having an obsession with the customer'. Presumably, this means they follow the customer everywhere, go through their dustbins and leave weird notes under their windscreen wipers. If you felt that your local butcher was obsessed with you as a customer, you might think twice about asking for a pork chop. The most laughable notion is 'Legendary Customer Service'. This can only mean that customer service was something that happened in the dim and distant past and no one remembers much about it anymore.

If we're honest, customers don't know what they want until they get it. There certainly weren't any big customer campaigns demanding a two-in-one shampoo and conditioner. Customers only know three things: they want things smaller, quicker, and cheaper. The oldest phrase to do with customers is. 'The Customer is always right.' Most people don't get anything else right in life so why should they suddenly be omnipotent when they go shopping? Customers – you can't live with them, you can't live without them – but you can take them for every penny they've got.

IT'S CALLED LEGENDARY BECAUSE EVERYONE'S HEARD ABOUT IT BUT NO-ONE'S EVER SEEN IT

CUSTOMER SERVICE

KEY LEARNINGS

- **Money can't buy you customers**
- **The customer is always right even when they're running out of your shop with armfuls of shoplifted merchandise**
- **A satisfied customer is one who's got what they're looking for at a reasonable price and has just been shagged senseless**

Five legendary customer service failures

Intended Service	Actual Consequence
Installation of Corby Trouser Press	National Grid shutdown
Pizza delivery	Multiple pile up on M25/M4 (£1 off for late delivery)
Opening current account	Three-week run on pound
Copywriting for Arabic pension brochure	Fatwa throughout Islamic world
Relaxing aromatherapy massage	Collapsed lung, renal failure, massive internal bleeding

SMALL BUSINESSES
❏ Where no one can hear you scream

The myth about starting your own business is that you work for yourself. You don't, you work for other people. If you really want to work for yourself, join a multinational company where you can happily work away for forty years with no noticeable effect.

Many stressed, aggressive people who work in big companies leave to start up their own businesses where they are totally dependent on stressed, aggressive customers in big companies. Naturally, small businesses often form informal associations for mutual self help and support. These are called Alcoholics Anonymous.

Setting up a business isn't about being your own boss, it's about being your own office junior. People who start a business are always banging on about how they used to do everything including cleaning the toilets. What they don't realise is that well over ten per cent of new businesses fail because too much time is spent cleaning the toilets.

The government is very helpful to small businesses and there are all sorts of enterprise schemes and advice centres to get you up and running and strong enough to withstand crippling taxation. When people who run their own businesses have trouble getting to sleep they dream about European employment legislation which says they mustn't work more than six hours a day without compulsory siestas and professional counselling.

Small businesses can be divided into those that have a van and those that have a shop. It's a rule of thumb that if you're successful in a van you

can go onto a shop because people will come to you. However, if you find yourself starting in a shop and ending up in a van you're in trouble, especially if you're in the restaurant business.

KEY LEARNINGS

- **The first sign of success in a small business is when you feel you can take a holiday**
- **Ninety per cent of small businesses fail during the owner's first holiday**
- **The definition of a small business is if your coffee cup can cover your order book**

Ten hairdressers that closed shortly after opening

1　Fringe Benefits
2　Hair today gone tomorrow
3　Scalpers
4　The Snip for Men
5　Wash and Blow
6　Clip Round the Earhole
7　Shear Indulgence
8　Parting is Such Sweet Sorrow
9　Edwina Scissorhands
10　Oi slaphead!

THE 100 CAST IRON COMMANDMENTS FOR TOTAL LIFE FULFILMENT

Every self improvement book ever written distilled into one easy-to-use, fully comprehensive guide to everything that's important in life.

TEN CAST-IRON WAYS TO HAVE AN EXHILARATING ACTION PACKED LIFE

1 Decide what's important to you and ditch the rest
2 Don't worry about things you can't change
3 Enemies have a hold on you – let them go
4 Invest in your education, skills and fitness
5 Don't get into debt, drugs or draylon
6 Be tough on yourself and gentle with others
7 In adversity hold tight and learn fast
8 Be bloodthirsty in one thing in your life
9 Change yourself and then change the world
10 Dream with your eyes open

TEN CAST-IRON WAYS TO ORGANISE YOURSELF FOR RAPID DECISIVE ACTION

1 Start work half an hour earlier
2 Work in small digestible chunks
3 Think in the morning, do in the afternoon
4 Guard your diary against unwelcome intruders
5 Get organised before you get an organiser
6 If you're not adding value, delegate
7 Don't go to a meeting without a timed agenda
8 Travel only if you'll return richer or happier
9 Keep your desk and your conscience clear
10 Plan tomorrow but act today

TEN CAST-IRON WAYS TO TAKE THE BUSINESS WORLD BY STORM

1   Concentrate on what you do best
2   Be enthusiastic – it's contagious
3   Talk to people with experience
4   Take short-term pain for long-term gain
5   Under-promise and over-deliver
6   When you're ready, take the big risk
7   Time wasters shorten life. Avoid them
8   The harder you fall, the harder you become
9   When they can't do without you, do without them
10 Never get personal unless it's personal

TEN CAST-IRON WAYS TO LEAD FROM THE FRONT AND COMMAND RESPECT

1   Passionately believe in your vision
2   Build a team that shares your vision
3   Work harder than anybody else
4   Keep your problems to yourself
5   Tell your team exactly what you expect of them
6   Listen to your team and respect their skills
7   Keep everyone informed and motivated
8   Give clear orders and make sure they happen
9   Share the profits
10 Very occasionally be ruthless

TEN CAST-IRON WAYS TO GET YOUR MESSAGE OVER AND KEEP IT OVER

1   Tell it like it is
2   If you really believe it, show it
3   Listen before you think before you speak
4   Headlines first, then the whole story
5   Consistency is the clearest message
6   If it really matters, do it face to face
7   Involvement is the best persuader
8   Encourage feedback and act on it
9   Little and often is better than once and for all
10 Communication works when something changes

TEN CAST-IRON WAYS TO THINK BIGGER, BETTER AND BOLDER

1 First create time and space for creativity
2 Read more, watch less
3 Seek out strange new people and ideas
4 Change your mind and the way you use it
5 Ambush ideas where no one's looking
6 Make the new connection
7 If it ain't broke fix it anyway
8 Try fresh words, numbers and colours
9 Unlock the simple from the complex
10 Give people what they never knew they wanted

TEN CAST-IRON WAYS TO MAKE WALLET-BENDING MONEY

1 Work harder, smarter and faster
2 Improve your skills
3 Cut costs which aren't useful or enjoyable
4 Always get a better quote
5 Chase debtors to hell and back
6 Stop adding and start multiplying
7 Get performance-related pay and then perform
8 For a big salary rise, change company
9 For really big money, own the company
10 Have something worth spending money on

TEN CAST-IRON WAYS TO BEAT THE HELL OUT OF STRESS

1 Say thank you, but no thank you
2 If it's not worth doing, don't do it
3 Never take your work home
4 Jealously guard your time and privacy
5 Simplify everything you do
6 Get ahead and stay ahead
7 Relax your body and your mind will follow
8 Eat well, enjoy friends, read in the bath
9 Indulge in regular rippling orgasms
10 Relax, worse things happen in the bikini area

TEN CAST-IRON WAYS TO MAKE LOVE LIKE YOU MEAN IT
1 Make love to the right person
2 Get the kissing right and the rest will follow
3 Watch your elbows
4 Dress to be undressed
5 Do what comes naturally
6 Have sex first then enjoy the foreplay
7 Continuously innovate
8 Do regular customer satisfaction surveys
9 Leave gymnastics in the gym, but try the leotard
10 There are prizes for coming second

TEN CAST-IRON WAYS TO AVOID BEING A TOTAL BASTARD
1 Listen
2 Be generous with your talents
3 Be nice to other people even behind their back
4 Hurting other people hurts you more
5 If it feels wrong, it is wrong
6 Take time to say thank you
7 Love, support and protect your family
8 Don't wait to be asked
9 You can't take it with you, so put it back
10 Clear your conscience before you go to bed

~ CHAPTER 6 ~

CARS, BIKES AND PLANES

The journey of a thousand miles starts with a single step.
So make sure you don't step in anything.

Sun Tse Zhoa ~ Sixth-century Chinese trainee philosopher

BUSINESS DRIVING
❑ Putting your foot down

On your average weekday there are two types of car drivers on Britain's motorways. There are pensioners visiting other pensioners and there are sales reps who have three calls to make in a day and 500 miles between them. If you suddenly find yourself being flashed by a car so close behind you that you can see the driver's nostril hair, you can be fairly sure that it isn't a pensioner in a desperate rush to visit another pensioner.

Driving at 110 mph on the motorway is quality time for the rep. It's a chance to call their friends, have a bite to eat, change their shirt and relax with a good book. Occasionally smaller cars stray into the fast lane driven by people who do less than 60,000 miles a year. This means reps have to brake hard to get down to eighty miles an hour and close enough to your back bumper for you to understand just how badly you're holding up the national economy by trespassing in their lane.

When you are a rep there are only two cars you are allowed to drive and they are a Ford Mondeo or a Vauxhall Vectra. Both cars are sold with a jacket already hanging up in the back seat. Other than that you can always recognise a rep's car by the complete lack of personal touches.

That's because you can't buy stickers that say 'I've seen the Lions at Longleat and sold them a photocopier'.

Driving for hours on the motorway with your body in one position means that your body can stiffen up and lead to dangerous and painful cramps. To combat this you can either get out and walk around (which you can do at any time on the M25) or you can do some in-car aerobics. This involves cutting up people and then flicking V signs at them, alternating with intensive sessions of nose picking. You can also hang one arm out of the window for no apparent reason with your shirt sleeve rolled up just far enough to hang your Rolex out. This is great until your whole arm gets ripped off by another Mondeo passing at 120 mph.

KEY LEARNINGS
- **There are no reps in slow lanes**
- **Overtake a rep and you sever his manhood**
- **Reps only drive cars you can unlock from the other side of the car park**

Ten ways to personalise your Vectra for maximum pulling power

1   Paint your name in Humbrol enamel on your door
2   Soak your upholstery in Blue Stratos
3   Have a giant, furry scrotum hanging from your rear-view mirror
4   Jack up back axle and fit low profile whitewall tyres.
5   Crochet your own lime green seat covers
6   Put the first four bars of 'Ride of the Valkyrie' on your horn
7   Convert your engine to run on Golden Virginian Benzene mix
8   Ask your local welder to fit gull wing Delorean doors
9   Urinate on each wheel
10 Buy personalised number plate IMA G1T

OFFICE CAR PARKS
❏ Finding your personal space

Office car parks are all built to a rigid standard which requires that they have ten per cent fewer spaces than cars. This allows people to indulge their flair for eccentric parking by leaving their cars in loading bays, flower beds and ornamental fountains.

There's always one space left in the car park and that is next to the big metal bins. Unless you drive an Austin Allegro don't park there. Those bins always have one dodgy wheel (as opposed to the Allegro which has a minimum of four). It's impossible for dustmen to empty the bins without doing at least a thousand pounds' worth of damage to surrounding cars (except for the Austin Allegro which you can write off totally and still do less than £10 worth of damage).

If your company has lots of sales reps who all drive Vauxhall Vectras there's a real danger that you'll drive off in the wrong car and only realise your mistake when you're stuck in a five mile tail back on the M62 with only 'The Best of Bonnie Langford' for company.

Just because you work in a city centre office with no parking doesn't mean you can't drive to work. Some people get their secretaries to feed the meter all day at a rate equivalent to £40,000 a year. Others will strip their BMW down to its component parts, keep it in a box under their desk and reassemble it at the end of the day, rather than take a bus.

There are balding men in their late fifties whose lives are dedicated to repeating the phrase, 'You can't park here'. The worst of these are armed with huge stickers that say 'You are illegally parked' that they slap on your windscreen with industrial strength adhesive. These men deserve pity not anger. At the end of the day they'll be the ones driving the snappy, head turning Austin Allegro.

KEY LEARNINGS
- He who parks last parks longest
- Traffic wardens are not the same thing as parks police
- Clamps have an instinctive attraction to BMWs

SPACE MANAGEMENT
❏ Navigating the corporate car park

The reason why bosses get to work first is because they've got such huge cars and fat necks that they have to park first without any reversing and manoeuvring. It's left to the Ford Fiesta brigade to squeeze into the tiny little gaps the senior managers leave behind. If you use reverse gear more than five times to get into a space you probably shouldn't be parking there. Remember, it's no good sitting there in the world's smallest gap feeling all pleased with yourself if you then can't open the door.

Some people, usually sales reps, block you in and leave their keys at reception. Naturally they are the same people that have fixed every kind of immobiliser and security device to their Vauxhall Vectra so that people won't steal it and undermine their masculinity. That's why when you attempt to unlock it and move it you won't get within five yards of it before enough sirens are going off to make anyone over sixty head for their air raid shelters.

Company car parks can still be very hierarchical with special places reserved for Chairman, Director, etc. You can guarantee your own spot with a sign saying Office Nerd or you can have the Chairman's spot by replacing his sign with 'Official Receiver'. Occasionally the best spot in the car park is reserved for Employee of the Month. If you walk to work or take the bus you can guarantee that you'll be employee of the month about seven times a year so the spot is kept clear for the Chairman. In some car parks you will see registration plates attached to the wall to allocate spaces. In fact these are usually number plates embedded in the wall by extremely bad drivers. Finally, don't forget that if you work in the office past eight in the evening on a regular basis, you are legally entitled to a residents' parking permit.

KEY LEARNINGS
- **Convert your car to a mobile breast-screening clinic and you can park anywhere**
- **Anywhere where there are breasts that is**
- **Try not to spend the whole day screening**

OFFICE CYCLISTS
❑ A pack of back pedallers

People who cycle to work think they have a God-given right to chain their bikes to their desk, sweat like a parrot and wander round the office with their gonads crushed like an old sandwich in their Lycra shorts. In the winter they leave their sodding lights everywhere and have nasty stalactites of ice clinging to their nasal hair. No wonder they never make it past the first rung on the corporate ladder.

In the old days cycling to work was fairly respectable. Men rode large black bicycles, with wicker baskets for their briefcases, and used sturdy wooden cycle clips to keep their pinstripe suits in order. Women did exactly the same except they rode side saddle. Nowadays people who trundle to work along a quiet cycle lane tog themselves up as if they were cycling up the North face of the Eiger. Their bikes have twenty-four gears out of which they only ever use the traditional Sturmey Archer selection – stiff, fairly stiff and not very stiff at all. The wheels work on the same principle as Clark's Commando shoes – the bigger the tread the tougher the wearer.

Aggressive urban cyclists view all cars as Panzers driven by the SS which is why they only use roads as a last resort and are much happier speeding along pavements, through shops and up large sewage pipes. Gone are the days of the little tinkling bell on the handlebars. Urban cyclists now have these special fog horns that would make an oil tanker think twice about turning left, let alone some old boy in a Metro. Fortunately, most of these cyclists are so horrifically ugly they are required by law to wear large face masks so as not to frighten elderly motorists and small children.

IT'S GOT A SPECIAL BACK PEDALLING DEVICE FOR ACCOUNTANTS

KEY LEARNINGS
- **Cyclists caused the great depression in the Thirties**
- **Bicycle pumps are one of the major causes of inflation**
- **The business cycle regularly causes massive unemployment**

Ten reasons why cyclists shouldn't be allowed to work in offices

1 They're all cheerful, red-faced and healthy
2 They take twelve minutes to get to work
3 They leave their bike lights everywhere
4 They arrive in a sweat and gently rot all day
5 They chain their bikes to the £1m Henry Moore sculpture
6 They pack their genitals in sweat-soaked Lycra
7 They can't give you a lift home when you're pissed
8 They won't work on any document that mentions the word 'car'.
9 They think excessive body hair is natural and attractive
10 They're all dangerous eco-radicals bent on the destruction of capitalism

CONFERENCES
❑ The power of coming together

Conferences are the business equivalent of going for a curry. Everyone thinks having one is a fantastic idea, but you always end up drinking too much, talking bollocks and feeling sick for days afterwards. One of the things that contributes to this queasiness is the themes used for conferences. Ninety per cent of conferences have the theme 'Simply the Best' or 'Playing to Win'. If conference themes bore any relation to reality at least one in three would be 'We're Up Shit Creek'.

The best conferences of all are sales conferences. This is where sales reps are called in from the country's motorway service stations and join together in a rollercoaster ride through the heights of passion and depths of emotion that go with the launch of a new brand of toilet cleaner. Many of these conferences require an overnight stay in the local hotel. This naturally leads to some frantic bedroom hopping by people who would be shocked and disgusted if they found their children doing the same thing while they were away.

Speakers vary in quality at conferences. There are some, generally from the IT department, who lose their audience somewhere in the phrase 'Good morning ladies and gentlemen'. 'If you do happen to be

THE FUTURE HAS NEVER BEEN BRIGHTER FOR THE COMPANY. SADLY MOST OF YOU WON'T BE AROUND TO SEE IT

BUILDING TOMORROW TOGETHER

awake during their speech, listen out for the phrase, 'but seriously'. This will be your only indication that a joke has been attempted. The Chief Executive's speech is often a high point of the conference in that things tend to go rapidly downhill after they've finished. Chief Executives generally talk about working smarter not harder which is a phenomenal waste of time because everyone in the audience knows that if they could work smarter they certainly wouldn't be working where they are now.

To add glamour to conferences celebrities are often invited to make guest appearances. They have to be booked well in advance and this often results in fiascos like a Scottish football manager talking about 'Playing to win'.

KEY LEARNINGS
- **Never speak at a conference unless you're spoken to**
- **Unless you're in an audience of 1,000, don't heckle the Chairman**
- **In five years' time you shouldn't be going to a Vision 2000 conference**

Top conference themes

1 Going for Gold
2 Simply the Best
3 Vision 2000
4 Everyone's a Winner
5 We are the Champions
6 Up Where We Belong
7 One Vision
8 Raising our Game
9 Building Tomorrow Together
10 Raising our Standard

78 *Raising our Trousers*
143 *We're neck deep in cack*
345 *You're going home in an ambulance*

PRESENTATIONS

❏ Coping with total silence and blank incomprehension

Giving a speech in front of a large business audience is as much fun as having your wisdom teeth removed by way of your rectum. Anything you can do to prepare in advance will lessen the agony. The first thing to do is ask yourself what you really want to say. If the answer to this is, 'I hate you, I hate you, I hate you!' it might be better if you didn't give a speech.

Prepare for a speech by producing an outline of what you want to say on a single sheet of paper. Then sketch out a conceptual framework to convey that message. Then throw the piece of paper away and write down every joke you've ever heard. Humour is a very useful way to help establish a rapport with the audience and what better way to announce a major programme of redundancies than with a string of dirty jokes.

A speech should last about the same time as a middle manager takes to make love. So about three bullet points should do it, followed by seven sides of closely typed apologies. Audio-visual support is a must in longer presentations. Really great speeches start with a joke, go straight into half an hour of completely gratuitous video clips of great sporting moments, and then end with instructions of how to get to the bar.

Statistics should be kept to an absolute minimum. Eighty-four per cent of people find that fifty-six per cent of speeches with more than forty-five per cent statistics are seventy per cent dull. If you have to use them, make them up to be really interesting such as eighty-four per cent of Sales Directors are or would like to be trans-sexual (that's actually true but you get the picture). When people check up on your dubious statistics afterwards, blame the person who made the slides.

Speeches are written to be heard rather than read, so it's fine to use more colloquial phrases such as, 'Wake up you bastards'. Finally, the golden rule of speechmaking is tell your audience what you're going to say, say it, and then run off the stage to a waiting car.

KEY LEARNINGS
- **Never speak from a lectern taller than you are**
- **Have a witty put down for hecklers such as, 'You're fired'.**
- **Ask your partner how boring you are and then double it. That's how boring you will be**

HOTELS

❏ All the comforts of home for the price of a second mortgage

Many business travellers claim that hotels are homes from home. With all due respect, that's utter nonsense because hotels are nothing like home. For a start you get a bed the size of a squash court that could still have the previous occupant in and you'd be none the wiser. The pillows on the bed are made of some sort of high pressure foam that won't let your head sink into it unless you're wearing a lead lined night cap. New smart technology means the hotel always knows who you are and what you're doing so that when you switch on the television in bed a little message pops up, 'Good Evening Mr Hollingsworth, thank you for choosing The Late Night Sleaze Channel'.

Things that everyone has at home cause great excitement in hotel rooms: 'Look, there's a little kettle, that's fantastic!' For women the most essential part of any hotel is the hair dryer. Sadly most hotel hair dryers have the power of an old man's dying breath. Also beware of the mini bar in your room. This is the most profitable part of the whole hotel and just opening the door adds at least two digits to your bill.

In good hotels, room service arrives in your room in seconds whether you want it or not. Getting them out of your room is another matter as they will lurk around for ever asking pointless questions like 'Have you come far?' until you empty out your wallet for a tip. This makes breakfast in your room extremely difficult as there's nothing worse than trying to suavely tip someone when you're half comatose and stark naked.

The one thing that will get someone in your room faster than room service is hanging out the 'Do Not Disturb' sign. This tells the voyeurs on the hotel staff when and where to burst in, causing maximum embarrassment to you and maximum enjoyment for them.

Most hotels these days operate an express checkout system. This is where you check out so fast that you forget your camera, your trousers and your briefcase full of vital business documents.

KEY LEARNINGS
- **It's impossible to enjoy a hotel room alone**
- **Only rock stars and Finance Directors trash hotel rooms**
- **A mini bar gin and tonic costs more per unit than frankincense**

AIR TRAVEL
❏ The secrets of upward mobility

The best part of business is travelling business class because it makes you feel incredibly important, business-like and tough. It also gives you an immediate and immense disdain for people who are not travelling in business class. These other people are found in economy and are usually referred to as 'cargo' or 'zoo class' or 'slum clearance'. There is also a subtle contempt for people who travel first class who must be either too rich to work for a living or international bankers which amounts to the same thing.

Business flyers collect frequent flyer points like they used to collect football cards. This is a bit of a mystery because business flyers are always complaining how much they hate flying and are bored to tears by it, while at the same time collecting like mad to claim their free eighteen-hour flight to Alaska.

If you have an Executive Club card it will record every conceivable preference from wing seat or aisle seat, lamb or pork for dinner, camp or matronly cabin crew. Executive lounges at airports are also something to get terribly excited about as they're packed with free papers worth well over 30p, all the mineral water your bladder can hold and all the executives with shiny trouser bottoms your heart desires.

Travelling business people are enormously important and rightly demand that they be in all forms of communication at all times. They insist on having phones, faxes, and mid-air e-mail so that they can let all their friends stuck in the office know the moment they have been offered a free hot towel.

Sadly some companies have a policy that you can only travel business if your flight is over four hours. This might explain why the person sitting next to you in business has just flown from Manchester to London via Moscow.

KEY LEARNINGS
- **Business people like to travel as close as possible to the pilot's bottom**
- **You're a frequent flyer when you have to show your passport before your partner lets you in the house**
- **Never put a blue executive club card on your briefcase when you're travelling business – it's an admission of corporate impotence**

INTERNATIONAL BUSINESS
❏ Working with alien life forms

It's one of the big mysteries in corporate life how big European multinationals operate successfully when most of their meetings involve people from countries that have little in common other than a shared distaste for the Spice Girls. It's especially mysterious given the fact that a for some reason everyone in these meetings tries as hard as they can to conform to their most grotesque national stereotypes. Nothing makes the French more French than when they are sitting between the Germans and the British. And should an American be in the meeting, then all the Europeans suddenly become walking repositories of thousands of years of culture, heritage and sophistication.

In these meetings the French will always insist on discussing the philosophical purpose behind everything, even if the meeting is about developing new worming pills for cats. The Germans will then tell the meeting in exhausting detail how they do things in Germany and why it would be better for Europe in general if everyone did it their way. As soon as the Belgians or Dutch say anything the Germans and the French will immediately start talking amongst themselves and work out a cosy solution that suits them both. Meanwhile the Italians will be sitting very carefully to make sure they don't put unnecessary creases in their suits and then will suddenly get very excited about a small point and threaten to walk out. The British will be very reasonable and understanding, make lots of jokes and find themselves at the end of the meeting holding the wrong end of the stick and completely isolated.

In fact these multinational meetings are very like the European Community in miniature. All parties try to get along for the sake of economic progress but really everyone wants to go home where things are done properly and you can get a decent sausage.

KEY LEARNINGS
- **Don't trust the Germans further than you can throw a large sausage**
- **Don't trust the French further than you can throw the leg of a small frog**
- **Don't trust other European types further than you can throw a jar of pickled cabbage**

HOLIDAYS

❏ Forget all you know about business in three seconds on the beach

For many people, the working year takes the form of four weeks' holiday with a forty-eight-week waiting period. Going on holiday is like working in advertising in that you get paid for sitting round doing nothing and forgetting about work for weeks at a time.

In the old days you used to know when somebody had been on holiday because they came back brown. These day, thanks to sunbeds, people slowly get brown before they go on holiday. The only thing that tells you they've actually been away is the fact that they suddenly come into the office wearing a strapless white dress to show off their tan. This can be rather disturbing when you're used to seeing them in a suit and tie.

People spend hundreds of pounds getting away from work and then spend all their time writing back to everyone in the office. Postcards back to the office generally have a rather nasty picture on with something crude scribbled over the top in biro. If you find yourself on the beach writing a postcard to your boss, you obviously haven't travelled far enough, relaxed enough or drunk enough. Unless of course the back of the postcard says, 'Dear Mr Howden, I'm marrying Zorba, so you can stuff your pension.'

Presents brought back from holidays are either little straw donkeys, little metal camels or little wooden elephants, unless you've been to the English Riviera where you can buy a little beach scene in a plastic dome which, when shaken up, covers itself in oil, litter and vomit. It takes about a year before you can throw away any of these little gifts without offending anybody, which is just in time to have it replaced by the next piece of cheap tropical schlock.

KEY LEARNINGS
- **Never take your work on holiday**
- **Never take your holiday photos into work**
- **Leave any company that calls you back from holiday**

~ CHAPTER 7 ~

DESKS, CHAIRS
AND POT PLANTS

Life is a game of musical chairs and no one sits pretty for long.
Brian Jenner ~ Twentieth-century American Dead Beat Poet

DESKS
❏ The life in front of you

You can tell everything you need to know about a person by the state of their desk. A desk covered in papers and reports and unfinished sandwiches means that you are an inefficient, fly-blown slob who should be sacked. A sparkling clean desk with nothing on at all means that you are an inefficient, fly-blown slob who has just been sacked. Untidy desks have three mandatory items: a slice of old Pizza whose topping is now a rare form of fungus, an order for £1 million of urgent business and a suicide note from the cleaner.

A good way of deciding whether your desk is untidy is to wait until the phone rings. If you can hear it but you can't see it, then your desk probably needs more than a light dusting. Some companies run a clean desk policy, which means that no one can leave work unless their desk looks like the flight deck of the *Ark Royal*. In practice, policies on clean desks usually translate into full drawers.

There are still a significant number of people who have framed photos on their desks. There should be a rule that photos of loved ones should only be taken when they've got red eyes and treble chins as this would encourage people to stay at work longer. People who work in intensely competitive environments often have photos of their opposite number in their competitors' firms. These have to be taken down if ever loved ones visit the office or they might get the idea that in fact they have been having a parallel relationship with a mean looking man with a moustache. Companies with a seriously competitive edge have a framed P45 on everyone's desk.

You can tell a lot about the company you work for by the desks it has. If your desk has a wooden lid and a little ink well in the corner, your company is unlikely to be at the cutting edge of the technological revolution. On the other hand if your desk looks like Houston Ground Control you're probably at the cutting edge of British technology and therefore almost certainly facing imminent redundancy.

KEY LEARNINGS

- **Fifty per cent of Finance Directors have a closer physical relationship with their desks than their partners**
- **Never completely clear your desk in case it is given to someone else to use**
- **When you can't see an inch of your desk for paper, change jobs**

Ten sure-fire signs your company's in the big league

1 It doesn't have Wigan anywhere in its name
2 MD has side parting in grey hair and one-syllable first name
3 You're more than fifteen promotions from the top
4 Trees in reception are larger than the ones outside
5 You don't have to explain who you work for
6 It works hand in glove with repressive regimes worldwide
7 You've never seen the directors' floor
8 Property value of the HQ is worth more than Wales
9 You have offices in more countries than the United Nations
10 When the company builds something, the Queen opens it

OFFICE PERSONALISATION
❏ Express yourself on the wall

The more anonymous offices become, the more people like to personalise their own little corners. In advertising you mark out your territory by urinating in your rubbish bin and throwing coloured marker pens at anyone in a suit. Normal people have to do it with subtle touches like a little poem, a favourite picture or a multi-coloured hand-knitted cosy for their entire desk and computer.

It always feels a lot more homely when you're allowed to have a radio on at work. Bosses who decide if radios are allowed should remember that the preferred station will be Noise FM and the preferred volume slightly louder than the heavy industrial process it accompanies. Remember also that in an office environment the chosen station might be Melody FM, so make sure the radio has a built-in alarm function to wake everyone at regular intervals.

Aside from mechanics working in small garages in Cumbria, men don't have pin-up calendars any more because they are all totally liberated from that sort of patronising sexist oppression. Instead they have moody, evocative, impressionistic black and white photographs, generally of naked women. Many working women love pin-ups and create huge colour montages of River Phoenix, Keanu Reeves and Antonio Banderas. This is actually rather insensitive as men in the office with ordinary names can find this quite threatening.

Some people have little funny stickers in the office. A favourite one is, 'You don't have to be mad to work here but it helps'. If you work as a receptionist for a psychiatrist it's probably best not to display that one too prominently. Another one popular in smaller companies is, 'The impossible we do today, miracles take a little longer'. The third unpublished line of this is, '...but normal orders take three months and get smashed to bits on delivery'.

KEY LEARNINGS
- If you really want to personalise your desk, make it smell
- A picture of your boss on your desk will make sure you go home on time
- Never have more than six pictures of children on your desk

OFFICE CHAIRS
❑ When you're sitting down, no one can kick your ass

There are two chairs in the Chairman's office. One is four foot wide, is made from the hide of a Charolais bull and looks like the palm of King Kong. This is not the one you sit in when you go for your annual carpeting. Your chair is the little plastic one which forces you to sit bent double and is on the point of complete collapse, which is exactly the feeling it's supposed to induce.

Big boardrooms generally have lots of huge swivel chairs. If it's your first board meeting, you won't make much of an impression if the rest of the board walk in and you're spinning round in your chair playing Magic Roundabout, especially if you then stagger across the room and throw up into the Chairman's wastebasket.

A few years ago special back chairs were introduced which you knelt in and which kept your spine at the perfect angle. These never really took off in the business community because if you suddenly had a fit of confidence and tried to swing your feet up on to the desk, you ripped your legs out of their sockets and found yourself in traction for the rest of the financial year. Secretaries have always had adjustable chairs so they won't get repetitive strain injury when they're on the phone to their friends for the best part of eight hours.

Beware offices with sofas. You are either in the personnel department where they like to make you comfortable while they fill out your P45, or you're in an advertising agency where they like to make you comfortable before showing you a creative campaign that could have been written by a chimp in a flotation tank.

When you start a new job, always check your chair very carefully. If it has straps on the arms and legs and a little electrode cap that fits neatly over your head, you might find the job a little too stimulating.

KEY LEARNINGS
- **If you can't stand the heat don't sit in the hot seat**
- **If you want to be in the driving seat, you've got to pass the driving test**
- **There are no long-haul flights by the seat of your pants**

POT PLANTS
❑ Sustainable business growth

Plants are to offices what goalkeepers are to football. They look ridiculous and their only function is to get in your way. Fortunately, out of the nation's seven million office plants, 4.5 million are currently dead or terminally ill. Most die of passive smoking because every cigarette stubbed out in a pot plant takes three weeks off its life – except for tobacco plants which absolutely thrive on it. Office plants are among the hardiest in the world because, apart from smoking twenty a day, they are fed on a diet of coffee, tea, oxtail soup and an annual dose of Christmas party urine. They also have to cope with the gardening efforts of the cleaners who give them a daily spray of Pledge to keep them looking nice.

There is one very healthy and beneficial aspect to pot plants. They take in noxious gases and recycle them as valuable oxygen. In this respect they are completely the opposite to the boys who work in the post room who take in valuable oxygen and recycle it as noxious gases.

Plants grow if you talk to them nicely, which is why plants in Personnel Departments do so well. This also explains why so many bosses have stunted little Bonsai trees on their desks. If you are going to have a pot plant, choose carefully. Your corporate image will not be enhanced if your desk is home to a neatly potted turnip.

Some offices get carried away with pot plants and working in them is like doing a tour of duty in Vietnam. If you find yourself going to work wearing khaki shorts and swinging a machete, your company is probably overdoing it. There are people who spend more time tending their pot plants than they do working. After a while bosses tend to notice this, especially if you have a thick layer of grass covering your desk, an attractive herb garden and an ornamental fountain feature.

KEY LEARNINGS
- **Feedback is the fertiliser of personal growth**
- **Prudent pruning now, gives great growth later especially in the bikini area**
- **Egos grow faster under a thick layer of bullshit**

Ten office plants and their natural habitats

Venus Flytrap	Reception
Rubber Plant	Stationery cupboard
Giant Redwood	Sales
Floribunda Exotica	Marketing Department
Slimy ground fig	Corporate Communications
Stenchwort	Warehouse
Single potted pansy	Library
Severely pruned Bonsai tree	Finance Director's office
Virtually extinct Slipper Orchid	Chief Executive
Dead Twig	IT department

CALL MAINTENANCE MISS CONDOR
I'VE DROPPED MY BISCUIT
IN MY TEA

COFFEE

❏ Releasing the hyper you

In primitive cultures manhood is sometimes tested by drinking a brew siphoned from the backside of the fanged dung bat. In our culture this has been replaced by the coffee vending machine. All the drinks have numbers such as White Without Sugar 402. This number generally refers to the atomic half life of what the machine dumps into your cup.

Vending machines fill up your cup to within one millimetre of the brim. The cup itself is so flimsy that the slightest pressure wangs it out of shape and spurts coffee down the office psychopath's neck. Even if you keep the cup together, by the time you reach your desk the top three layers of skin on your fingers will have been melted off.

If you're a smoker, nothing makes coffee taste better than a long drag on a cigarette. If you're a non-smoker nothing makes coffee taste worse, especially if you swallow the butt someone dropped in it earlier. Some people experience a sharp stabbing sensation in their eye when they drink coffee. This can easily be remedied by removing the spoon from the cup before drinking.

Anyone who works in an office will have noticed the strange gravitational pull between coffee and the document that you shortly have to present to your boss. Human reactions are never quicker than when a coffee is about to spill. At the last moment it can often be knocked clear of the document and straight into the keyboard of your computer.

In an open plan office there is a ritual where everyone waits hours for the first person to say 'Who wants a coffee?' That person then finds themselves in the kitchen for the rest of the day following the little chart that says 'Diane, white with two Nutrasweet and half an Orange Jasper'. Naturally everyone hates vending coffee, but there's one thing that everyone hates more and that's the 'I don't drink coffee, I'll have a rhubarb tea' brigade.

KEY LEARNINGS

- **Only losers like their coffee whipped**
- **Coffee keeps you working when your brain has gone home**
- **232 is well recognised as an office aphrodisiac**

Average office vending machine usage

Coffee, white no sugar	325
Coffee, white one sugar	298
Tea, white no sugar	264
Coffee, black no sugar	260
Hot Chocolate	251
Oxtail soup	87
Chocolate Oxtail	34
Water without cup	16
Remy Martin VSOP (Directors' Floor only)	12
Packet of 3 flavoured	69

Type of biscuit	Likely occupation
Boaster	Estate agent
Rusk	Social services
Fig roll	Persian carpet wholesaler
Rich shortie	Successful small businessman
Pink wafer	Design consultant
Garibaldi	Aging football manager
Jammie Dodgers	IT computer software salesman
Lemon Puff	PR
Orange Jaspers	Mobile phone salesmen
Rich Tea	Famous rap artist

CARPETS
❏ **Learn to love them because that's where you'll end up**

When you find yourself being carpeted by someone in senior management it's a very good opportunity to check out your company policy on carpets. If you look closely you will find that many companies think it's the height of good taste to have a carpet with their logo woven in. It's amazing just how many companies have an old coffee splodge as their corporate logo. Weaving the logo into the carpet is also to stop people taking a 100 square metre offcut for home use, although some people get a perverse thrill from having a British Tube Investment offcut in their bedroom.

Board level carpets tend to have a higher shag factor. The first reason for this is that there is very little wear on the carpet except for a little footpath between the desk and the mini bar. The second reason is that a shaggier carpet gives a more accurate approximation of the rough on the eighteenth hole for those vital practice shots.

Somewhere in every office there is a stack of eight spanking new carpet tiles. These are the spare ones that are put down immediately after any spillage on the carpet. 'Immediately' that is if anybody could remember where they were stored. In practice it's far easier to take the stained tile and replace it with a clean one by the office nerd's desk so that after a while he has a little moat of coffee stains round his desk that give the impression that he can't hold a coffee cup without flinging half of it on the floor.

Some modern offices cleverly colour code their carpets by department so that you always know exactly where you are. So for example the IT department would be green, the Marketing department orange and the Finance department would be concrete because carpets are a needless extravagance.

KEY LEARNINGS
- **The average office worker is allowed eight carpet tiles of space**
- **When carpet tiles are flying through the air, teamwork has broken down**
- **Seventy-six per cent of business failures occur in offices with brown carpets**

LIFT ETIQUETTE
❏ Going down in the office

Office lifts are mini laboratories for the study of human embarrassment. That's because it's generally very difficult to make polite conversation with someone who is within an inch of the farthest tendrils of your nasal hair and whose groin you are simultaneously jabbing with your briefcase. On the other hand some women find lifts an excellent place to give themselves a total makeover, highlight their hair and wax their bikini area in the space of ten floors. This may be very convenient for them, but it can be embarrassing for everyone else in the lift.

If you want to know whether a company is going up in the world you need look no further than its lifts. Any company where the walls of the lifts are carpeted is a company on the royal road to receivership; any company with glass lifts on the outside of the building is probably still reeling from the effects of colossal Eighties' embezzlement; and any company with more lifts than floors is unlikely to be much good at any sort of business.

In some quaint old lawyers' offices they like to retain the ancient wooden lifts with the metal cage doors that are so heavy that you can only open them if you're the sort of person who regularly bench presses over 300 pounds. Once inside you push the button and the lift hurtles upward at a floor every ten minutes. If you get stuck in one of these lifts never push the emergency button, as this just severs the hairy old rope that's holding the lift up.

New lifts have electronic voices that patronise you by saying 'Going up' when you've just got in at the ground floor. What would be better is a voice that said really useful things like, 'I'm afraid someone's just farted. Would the man in the green tie get out at the next floor for the convenience and safety of the remaining passengers.' Modern lifts also have extremely sensitive doors which can be held open by the frailest of old ladies. You have to wedge their whole body in sideways, but it can be done.

KEY LEARNINGS

- Newton's laws of physics do not apply to lifts
- When you go up to the Chairman's floor you still get a sinking feeling
- When you come back down you feel uplifted
  (if you've still got your job)

A GOOD RECEPTION
❏ The power of first impression

I f visiting a company is like a blind date, then the reception is where you get your first impressions. Of course dates are slightly different in that you don't normally take a number and wait until you're called. But dates and receptions are exactly the same in the amount of useless waiting around involved.

Some companies model their reception on conditions in *The Bridge on the River Kwai*. You're left in a dark room for hours, with nothing to eat or drink, not knowing what's going to happen to you and an evil-looking security man watching your every move. When you've reached breaking point someone friendly will call your name only to tell you that 'Mr Dart is running a little behind schedule, he's very sorry, but would you mind sitting there for another four hours.'

This is when you turn in desperation to the reading matter that's been left for you. The lowest of the low is a company newsletter. Life offers few things bleaker than a three-hour wait in the reception of a heavy engineering firm with the only reading matter a copy of *The Spanner*. Of course being too generous with the reading material can have the opposite effect. If you're visiting a firm that makes septic tank pumping systems, a quick flick through *Vogue* or *Country Life* might bring you dangerously close to a 'Stuff your septic tank pumping systems' state of mind.

When you visit another company you always have to go through the ritual of signing the visitors' book which would be better titled the 'Unwelcome intruders book'. You have to put down all your details of who you are, who you're seeing, what your trade secrets are and when you're going to be getting the hell out of their building. Remember when you're signing in to check for previous entries such as 'Official Receiver', 'Serious Fraud Office', or 'Communicable Diseases Unit'.

KEY LEARNINGS
- **Attractive receptionists mean big invoices**
- **At any given moment during the working day there are 1.2 million people waiting in business receptions**
- **Your contact will finally appear the moment you start to make a call on your mobile**

STAFF RESTAURANTS
❏ A foretaste of hell

I THINK I'VE GOT THE
FINANCE DIRECTOR'S
SANDWICH

In an office you know it's lunch time when your stomach starts making more noise than your boss. Getting away from the boss at lunch time is great as long as this doesn't mean going to the staff canteen. Canteen is short for 'Can't eat there without feeling nausea.'

In job advertisements you often see 'subsidised canteen' offered as some sort of inducement. Unless it's followed by 'free health insurance', steer clear of the job. English food has little to recommend it at the best of times and when you try to serve a meal at 30p a head it's not surprising that you end up with the culinary equivalent of trench foot on your plate.

Naturally shepherd's pie is a big favourite with canteens. For vegetarians they can take the meat out and call it country pie and for something really exotic they can add curry powder and call it dragon pie. Lasagne is shepherds pie with pasta instead of potato and ocean pie is shepherds pie with fish. This is normally served on Friday so that people will at least have the weekend to forget all about it.

These days a lot of catering is contracted out to customer-focused private catering companies. 'Customer-focused' means they don't take their eyes off you when you're helping yourself to chips in case you take too many and jeopardise the dividend for shareholders. Their big secret is 'portion control' which means instead of being able to slosh ketchup all over your lasagne, they give you one sachet to squeeze which yields up little more than a good-size blackhead.

In the old days there used to be a separate restaurant for executives. Nowadays it's all democratic and open plan and you can sit wherever you want, which of course happens to be any table which doesn't have any executives on.

KEY LEARNINGS
- **The average lunch in a canteen takes fourteen minutes**
- **The average pub lunch takes two hours fourteen minutes**
- **Successful companies locate a long way from pubs**

Top ten names for women who serve in staff restaurants

1 Maureen
2 Noreen
3 Doreen
4 Soreen
5 Canteen
6 Hasbeen
7 Shebeen
8 Easycleen
9 Halloween
10 Windscreen

CANTEEN

IT'S NOT JUST THE PLUM THAT'S DUFF

The office pecking order – your sandwich never lies

Your favourite sandwich filling	Where that puts you in the office
Cheese	Work experience
Cheese and tomato	Assistant to Junior Spod
Chicken salad	Junior Spod
Egg mayonnaise	Senior Spod
Chicken tikka	HR Director
Honey glazed ham and rocket	Secretary
Corned beef and mustard and lard	PA
Honey, oats and peanut butter	Receptionist
Vaseline and pecan nuts	Sales Executive
Colgate SR salsa and crispy bacon	Sales Manager
Weetabix and Pedigree Chum	Associate Sales Director
King prawns in gravadlax mousse	Sales Director
Royal jelly with garlic butter	Regional Sales Director
Apricot brisket with chocolate fudge glaze	National Sales Director
Gravadlax in lime and dill sauce	Vice President Sales
Alligator bisque in loganberry julienne	Managing Director
Roast swan in a beluga carapace	Chief Executive
Quinquereme of heron in a threatened species sauce	Chairman

~ CHAPTER 8 ~

PHONES, FAXES AND COMPUTERS

*Clarity of communication is the essential business lubricant,
if you get my drift.*

Karen Kimberley ~ Twentieth-century English communications guru and hammer thrower

TELEPHONE SALES
❏ The secrets of deep throat

More and more business is done over the phone. This is not necessarily a good thing if the person who answers the phone says, 'Good Morning this is National Services, my name is Charmaine, how can I help you?' These people are working to a tight script so it's always good for a laugh to put them off their stride with questions such as, 'Are you crying inside, Charmaine?'

Answering a phone in an office generally means speaking to a customer or your boss. As neither will call unless they want something, answering the phone will probably mean doing work. Rule Number One, therefore, is don't pick a phone up unless you know it's a social call. As you'll never know whether an incoming call is social or not, it's best to make a lot of pre-emptive outgoing social calls.

Managers always get terribly upset about unanswered calls and pretend that it could have been someone offering millions of pounds of new business. You know that's very unlikely because you've actually just had someone on the phone offering millions of pounds of new business and been so rude to him that he rang off. Managers try to improve telephone answering by instituting policies where you have to pick up any phone within five rings. Happily the policy doesn't say anything about slamming it back down immediately after picking it up.

Having more than one phone on your desk used to mean that you were enormously important. In fact the more your desk looked like the local telephone exchange the more important it meant you were. Not any more. Nowadays, if you're really important, a phone ringing on your desk is about as likely as a seagull landing on it. Instead you have teams of people screening your calls and anyone with an axe to grind is immediately transferred to the Customer Careline where they are patronised to death.

KEY LEARNINGS

- **Suzie Dowdall of Clapham is still holding on a call she made in the late Eighties**
- **Customers who insist on speaking to someone who can help should be put through to a psychiatrist**
- **Ninety per cent of customers ring off after five rings so it's worth waiting**

DIRECT LINE SERVICES
❏ The phone as business tool

B usiness is being revolutionised by direct line services. This is where you phone in and speak to someone who sounds like a cheerful speak your weight machine. One of the reasons they're so cheerful is that they have computers in front of them which store all your personal information. All they need is your postcode and they can tell you your inside leg measurement and the last time you passed wind. You can then order an airline ticket, a jumper or even a mortgage, sure in the knowledge that if you're not happy with anything you can phone them up again and get an engaged signal for a week and a half.

There are a lot of security procedures on the phone which generally involve asking you personal questions. The favourite one is, 'What is your mother's maiden name?' With the rise in the number of unmarried mothers this will have to change soon, perhaps to something like, 'Have you any idea who your father is?' If they start asking you questions such as 'Do you wear high-heeled shoes in bed?' they've probably gone past the security procedure to their own personal gratification procedure.

The most annoying part of ordering on the phone is that they repeat everything you say. When you've just told them that your name is Smith, they'll say, 'That's Sierra Mike India Tango Hotel,' as if they're speaking from Heathrow ground control. It's all you can do to stop yourself saying, 'I can't hold her, starboard engine's on fire!!' Before these direct line people finish, they always ask whether they can use your details 'to provide information on other services that might be of interest to you'. The correct response here is, 'Foxtrot Uniform Charlie etc.'

KEY LEARNINGS
- **Direct line operators can't cope with jokes**
- **So don't make any**
- **Or give them your bank details**

TELEPHONE TENNIS
❏ Smashing your opponent

If being put on hold is the telephone equivalent of a traffic jam, then calling any government department is the equivalent of a fifteen-mile tail-back on the M25. Sometimes you will hear the message, 'Your call is held in a queue and will be answered as soon as possible.' A literal translation of this is, 'You are now paying good money to be patronised by a machine'. After this you will be played some baroque music to soothe your nerves whereas 'You keep me hanging on' by the Supremes would be more appropriate.

Generally, the reason calls don't get answered is because people are always 'in meetings', which can mean anything from showing the

Japanese Board of Trade around the office to having a Fantasy Football update in the post room. However, if you're making the call and the person you want is 'in a meeting' you should always ask if it's an 'internal meeting'. If it is this automatically implies that their meeting is an utter waste of time and money and should be immediately interrupted as your plane for Buenos Aires is now boarding.

Phone manners are important and there's nothing more annoying than people who don't say goodbye and just hang up as if they're working in some sort of Chicago newspaper office. The trick with these oh-so-busy people is to phone them back immediately after they've hung up, say 'Goodbye' and then put the phone down. They'll soon get the hang of it.

One last word of warning. Don't start fancying someone on the phone just because they've got a velvety voice that crawls up your trouser leg. It is an immutable law of business that people who sound gorgeous on the phone turn out to be truffling ground hogs in real life.

KEY LEARNINGS
- **Never put the Chairman on hold**
- **Never put your phone down before your boss does**
- **Listen for the click before using the word 'wanker'**

MOBILE PHONES
❏ Should you use them on the loo?

The marvellous thing about mobile phones is that wherever you are, whatever you are doing, you can keep them switched off so no one will bother you. If you do use them, you can make calls from virtually anywhere. For example, around about mid morning you can call the office from underneath your duvet as long as your partner can make realistic motorway service station noises.

There are two places where everybody automatically hates you if your mobile rings – restaurants and funerals. In both cases it's best to give the impression that the call is so vital that you absolutely had to answer it. Say something like, 'Hello Mum, is Dad out of intensive care?' Of course this doesn't work if you're actually at your parent's funeral.

When mobile phones first came out, the only people to have them were estate agents or drug dealers. These days respectable people also have them. However, even if you're a district nurse and your mobile rings in public, people will still assume you're an estate agent, drug dealer or both, which is a shame because for many working women the mobile phone is vital for their safety and independence. For men, on the other hand, having a mobile is a chance to pretend you spend a lot of time working on oil rigs or other tough, remote locations, even if it rings when you are in the lingerie section of Marks and Spencer.

Of course, mobile phones are especially useful for anyone who spends a lot of time away from the office, most bosses for example. Many business people use their phones in their cars. Of course this is strictly forbidden unless you have a 'hands-free' set. Men tend to ignore this rule because they are used to driving virtually hands free while they excavate the inner recesses of their nostrils with one hand and fiddle with their genitals with the other.

KEY LEARNINGS

- If you disguise the ring of your phone to sound like the mating call of a rare curlew, don't be surprised to find birdwatchers following you home
- If you are making a call while on the loo, ring off before you flush
- If you have more than twenty numbers on your phone's memory, you've probably forgotten what your children look like

---

IT PEOPLE
❑ In the back of the net

The internet is like a hair net because if you are an elderly lady, they are both more than likely to be over your head. These days no one will take you seriously in business unless you have a website on the internet. That's why you have to spend half a million pounds setting out your company stall on a fully interactive computer site so that lonely pubescent boys from Arkansas can accidentally dip into it while surfing the net for rude pictures.

'Surfing the net' is much like surfing in the English Channel, because nothing happens for ages and then all of a sudden a wave sneaks up behind you and covers you with sewage. In the same way you can wait forever while your computer queues up to get onto a web site only to find that it's got the entertainment value of the test card. (Remember you don't need a wet suit to surf the net, unless you're a member of one of those weirdo 'special interest' user groups.)

When telling people your e-mail address over the phone you've got as much chance of them getting it right as you have of leaving your name correctly with a French telephone receptionist. With e-mail addresses getting the dots, dashes and slashes right is incredibly important so if you want to guarantee no one ever gets through to you, try this address: Hyphendot@dash.slash.dot.at.com.uk.

Of course e-mail on the net is absolutely fantastic if you have relatives in Alaska who are also on e-mail because you tap away to them for the cost of a local phone call and also give the impression to the rest of the office that you're doing some pretty intensive work on your computer. Don't try this if you work in advertising, as any sign of intensive work will mark you out as unsuitable for promotion.

KEY LEARNINGS
- **Imagine all the nerds in the world in one room; that's the internet**
- **What do you call the space between a frog's toes? A web site.**
- **No visitors to Charlie Trumpess's web site have ever returned**

THE INFORMATION SUPERHIGHWAY
❑ Using the pedestrian subway

Business is in the middle of a technological revolution so complex, so rapid and so complete that within a few years no one will understand anything. The fruits of this revolution are now on most people's desks. You know when you've got a piece of state-of-the-art technology on your desk because like all modern art, you stare at it for a long time without a clue what it's for.

Since no one else will speak to computer people, they have developed their own nerdy language: Groupware is when you've got Motorhead logos on your underwear, data warehousing is some sort of storage facility for eastern dried fruits and megabytes are those horrible red blotches on nerds' necks where they have snogged each other too hard. Hypertext sounds like output from PR companies, in fact it's text on screen that you can touch to make something happen. It works on the same principle as hyper people in the office – touch them and you get a smack in the mouth.

Virtual reality is like marketing. It seems real but there are too many unbelievable people doing bizarre things for anybody to take it very seriously. Interactive multimedia is like virtual reality except you don't wear it on your head. You can still do amazing things with it though, like look all round an aircraft, sit in the seats, call a steward, and all without ever taking off. Much like Air France in fact.

It's some consolation to know that behind every high-tech piece of office equipment there is a low-tech nerdy designer with mucus-clogged nostrils. The computer may be able to do a task in three minutes that once took three days, but it will also have an on/off switch that will take a team of micro-surgeons to locate. Frighteningly, the high-tech revolution has led to the emergence of a new kind of high-tech repairman. They tap in a few commands, inform you they've just

APPARENTLY IT'S WHAT PEOPLE USED BEFORE THE COMPUTER

rebuilt your hard drive and then send you an invoice with a bottom line that looks like a computer serial number.

KEY LEARNINGS
- By the end of the century computers will be five times more powerful than the human brain
- That's fifteen times more powerful than a marketing brain
- And as much fun at the office party as the entire purchasing department

---

BUSINESS LANGUAGE
❑ Explaining the bad taste in your mouth

I n business they say that 'people buy people'. That's not a reference to the slave trade but rather to the fact that people who like you are more likely to buy what you're selling. That's why business has developed its own language which sounds friendly on the outside but isn't on the inside.

For example you're often forced to deal with people in business who you would throw peanuts at in private. When these people make a suggestion the natural response is 'Shut up, you fathead'. In business this translates to 'Let me get back to you on that one', 'I'm glad we've got that on the table' or 'Let's park that idea and come back to it'.

Business life generally involves lurching from one crisis to another and naturally there are many phrases to cover this. Many are sexual in origin with projects being 'cock ups' or 'balls ups' or, increasingly, 'going tits up'. Bottoms also feature and a current hot phrase for a business disaster is 'my bum's in the custard'.

Giving criticism in business is a matter of finding a bush and then beating around it. In order not to hurt anyone's feelings you have 'friendly evaluation' which, like friendly fire, still hurts like hell. Friendly evaluations are based on what you would 'commend' and what you would 'recommend'. The sub-text of this is always 'I commend you to a recruitment agency' and 'I recommend you leave immediately'.

In negotiation on price there's usually only one thing you want to say and that's 'HOW MUCH?!!' This translates into, 'You've got some ambitious price parameters there. What's the stretch?' Finally, in business you can say exactly the same thing but completely alter the meaning by changing the word order: 'when can you do a meeting?', 'we must have a meeting' and 'it was nice to meet you'.

KEY LEARNINGS
- **Executive he speak with forked tongue**
- **Which is why he say 'fork off' a lot**
- **Best not trustum**

Management Jargon	Plain English
Environmentally conscious	Bribing Health and Safety inspectors
Passionate commitment	Unalloyed greed
Market leaders	Our reps have faster Mondeos than your reps
State-of-the-art technology	We've got a computer
Global leaders	No one else bothers
Profitable growth	Car park like Geneva motorshow
Young, growing company	Child labour
Shareholder value	We're being blackmailed by pension funds
Delighting our customers	We've finally made something that works
Continual innovation	Chaos
Teamwork	The buck goes round in circles
Obsession with the customer	Customer stalking and hostage taking
Learning organisation	Continual disastrous mistakes
Lean and efficient	Continual headcount reduction
Developing all our people	Exposing them to a cocktail of chemicals
Open and honest	That's a lie for a start
Responsive, flexible, dynamic	We'll do anything to survive
Exceeding expectations	Nasty surprises
First choice	Vice-like monopoly
Total commitment to quality	Upcoming sale of company to Japanese
Upholding the highest traditions of the company	Mad family with majority shareholding
Best of Breed performance	Dog-like lethargy
Creativity	Sloppy organisation
Integral part of community	Our toxins are absorbed by local people

COMPUTER APPLICATIONS
❑ Who do they apply to?

People who have a PC on their desk probably have more computing power at their disposal than the whole of Britain had twenty years ago. Sadly, our brains haven't developed at the same rate. Generally we only use about one per cent of our total computing power, which is roughly equivalent to the percentage brain power in use by your average advertising executive.

This is a shame because today's computer programmes can let you do all sorts of wizzy things. Word processing packages not only correct your spelling as you go along but can also give you auto formatted text for things you find yourself having to write over and over again such as indecent proposals, grovelling apologies, resignation letters, etc.

Spreadsheets are basically calculators with attitude. Financial Directors love them because you can set them up to tell you what impact one more portion of ketchup used in the canteen will have on the annual results of the whole company. The answer is absolutely nothing but setting up these kind of spreadsheets keeps Finance Directors quiet for months and that's got to be good news for everyone.

Databases are fantastic for making a list of all your customers and building up a very accurate profile of what their personal spending habits are. They're a valuable marketing tool and you can spend many happy hours setting one up as your customers try for hours to get through to your diverted phone. Companies like to trade databases and some are extremely valuable. For example the database of people who bought *The Best of Julio Iglesias* is very sought after because it's basically a list of people with more money than sense.

KEY LEARNING
- **The basic difference between a word processor and a food processor is that you can kiss a word processor without having your face sliced off by whirring blades**

Ten worst-selling computer programmes of all time

1　Virtual Family Christmas
2　3-D dredging
3　Rat dissection grand prix
4　Dyslexic word processing
5　Alimony spreadsheets
6　Prisoner time management system
7　Virtual internal examination
8　Cyber washing up
9　Computer crash simulator
10　We come in peace space game

THE FAX

❏ Separating fax from fiction

When you accidentally phone a fax it gives out a little screaming noise. This is the electronic equivalent of the inner scream everyone feels when they're interrupted by some idiot phoning them. Occasionally a fax will spew out pages of blank paper, like the fax equivalent of heavy breathing. This either means that someone has put their fax in upside down, or it's a summary of all the valuable work your advertising agency has done that year.

Early faxes had silly flimsy paper much like army toilet paper. (In fact the contents were often alarmingly similar.) This paper curled itself tighter than a Bedouin's slipper, came out in one long strand and took half the office to hold it down before you could read it. This was soon replaced by the plain paper fax which gave you ordinary A4 paper from a machine that only cost seven or eight times the price.

Most faxes have URGENT written on the top which means that if you receive one you must take it immediately with the utmost urgency and place it quickly and urgently in the big pile with all the other urgent faxes. Faxes also have a little warning at the bottom saying 'Only to be read by the addressee'. This is a warning that should you even just take a little peek at the contents you will get a flying visit by the Armed Unit of the Serious Fraud Squad. If you're worried about confidentiality and other people reading it, make the second page of your fax a big bold message saying, 'Mind your own business, fatty'.

Remember that faxes often have the name of who has sent it on the top. So if you're faxing in your CV to some top level company it won't make much of an impression if you get your local pizza restaurant to fax it in for you. Junk faxes are faxes that arrive during the night which advertise West End shows on the point of closure. The worst form of junk fax are those advertising cheap rates for fax paper because if it weren't for their junk faxes you wouldn't need to replace the paper every five minutes.

There are still people who send you a fax and then follow it up with a hard copy in the post. These are the same people who work something out on a calculator and then whip out an abacus to make doubly sure everything adds up. Fax back a copy of their hard copy to say you've got it and ask for an acknowledgement by post of their receipt of your fax.

KEY LEARNINGS
- **Faxes are like business valentines**
- **People love getting them**
- **And it doesn't matter who they're from**

Top ten office newsletters

Company	Newsletter
Westland Helicopters	Big Choppers
Exxon Oil	Life's a Beach
Union Carbide	Smoke Signals
Goldman Sachs	The Joy of Bondage
HMV	One Voice
Linklaters and Paynes Solicitors	Invoice
Reeves and Paine Undertakers	Hasta la Vista!
Alabama Department of Correction	Switched On
Interpersonal Skills Consultancy	Oi!
Shanks and McEwan	The Dirt

~ CHAPTER 9 ~

CONSULTANTS, NERDS AND CLEANERS

If truly there was nobility in work,
you'd find the nobility doing a lot more of it.
Theodore Wiggins ~ Eighteenth-century English muffin

WE CAN ENGAGE IN IDLE
CHIT CHAT IF YOU LIKE
BUT THE METER'S TICKING

CONSULTANT

CONSULTANTS
❏ More money than sense

A consultant is someone in business with an ego so large it takes more than one company to support it. At a personal level consultants work either by trying to inspire fear or trying to be friends. When they try to be friends is when they inspire the most fear. Management Consultants are much like Medical Consultants in that they're paid to keep a straight face while examining the shrivelled private parts of industry. Consultants often start with what they call a scoping exercise. This derives from the medical practice of getting you to drop your trousers and cough. The real point is to see how heavily your wallet hits the floor and to gauge how much can be removed from it later. The headquarters of big consultancy firms reek of expense. Just sitting in their reception has the same effect on your budget as cold water has on your gonads.

The acid test of a consultant is whether they can say, 'Everything's fine, we'll be off then'. No real consultant can. Instead they'll sell you a project that costs just enough to keep your profits suppressed to a level that requires almost continual consultancy.

All consultants claim to have worked with one successful company so they can say, 'At BA we looked very seriously at matrix management'. What they don't tell you is that they worked for BA as a student pulling chewing gum off seats in economy and the closest they got to matrix management was playing Connect 4 in the works canteen.

To be fair consultants do leave you with a nice report. This lists all the figures your company has ever produced, highlighting enough mistakes for your Financial Director to keep very quiet when it comes to paying the bill. Somewhere at the back of the report is a summary of recommended actions. The first one, in heavily disguised language, says, 'make more money or you'll be neck deep in cack'. The other, in clearer language, says, what you really need is another scoping study.

KEY LEARNINGS
- **Good managing directors select good consultants**
- **Because good consultants do your entire job for you if you pay them nicely**
- **And if they do a really good job you'll be promoted and be able to afford some even better consultants**

MARKETING
❏ Liberating the hidden power of mango

In marketing there is an unspoken rule which says, 'if it ain't broke fix it anyway'. That's why one day you'll nip into the shops for your favourite product only to find it says, 'Now with added mango.' This can happen to any product from carpet slippers to disposable nappies.

Gone are the days when you could sell a simple product. You now have to sell it with bells, whistles and widgets, in a luminous, foil-wrapped, bio-degradable, resealable, low-calorie, unleaded, easy-scoop, microwaveable, non-biological, galvanised, sustainable package with extra vitamins, fibre, minerals, anti-oxidants and nutritious gravy, with a life-time, no quibble, fully comprehensive, interest-free, fire and theft, sale or return, three for the price of two, buy now pay later guarantee, now with added mango, madam.

Naturally people are now hankering for the good old days when you could pop down to the grocer and buy a straightforward hogshead of butter, a cubit of flour and a quatrain of sugar, sure in the knowledge that the only additives would be a selection of insects, worms and microbiological nasties. In those good old days you didn't need tamper-proof tops either, because you knew if you got anywhere near anything worth tampering with, you'd get a thick ear.

When they're not adding something, marketing people are claiming better performance – often for their products. Toilet paper has been getting 'even softer' for about thirty years and, unless it started as slabs of granite, it must be reaching the limits of softness. At some point the marketing people will go into reverse and start claiming that each new roll is harder, firmer and more aggressive and they'll subtly change the advertising from a small puppy to a spiky looking armadillo.

KEY LEARNINGS
- **This little piggy went into marketing**
- **This little piggy stayed at home**
- **Which piggy do you prefer?**

Ten brand extensions too far

1 Armitage Shanks Eau de Toilet
2 Kentucky Fried Evening Wear
3 Preparation H Turnaround Cream
4 Lamborghini stair lifts
5 No Fear carpet slippers
6 Laura Ashley full strength chewing tobacco
7 Calvin Klein Cat Wormer
8 Rentokil Baby Bath
9 Clearasil Creamy Devon Custard
10 Cadbury Fruit and Nut Mental Health Plan

PR AGENCIES
❏ Mostly bad news

PR companies make their money by a simple formula. They scare the pants off major companies by talking about some X factor that could ruin their business and then charge a hefty retainer for making sure the X factor never happens. When it doesn't happen they claim a major victory and send you a series of celebratory invoices.

A very small part of what PR does is to help create awareness of your product. This they do by spending a fraction of their colossal retainer hiring a bunch of tired and emotional actors to hand out hastily prepared leaflets at your local railway station.

When choosing a PR agency remember that they work on a basis of the other form of PR, i.e. proportional representation. If they are representing a major oil company with a multi-million pound account, your little piece of business will be given to a student placement to do when they've finished making the coffee. A good rule of thumb is that you should never hire a PR agency that is better known than your own company, because if you do, that position certainly won't change.

At the vile, slimy end of PR is the publicist whose job is to keep your face in the media. This explains what became of the boy at school who made it his mission in life to keep flushing your head down the lavatory. Having your face constantly in the media is the psychological equivalent of having your face constantly in a food processor.

PR agencies are like advertising agencies in that they involve an almost continuous round of parties, lunches and general swanning about. The small but noticeable difference is that with an advertising agency you might have something to show for it at the end.

KEY LEARNINGS

- **If you want good publicity sack your PR agency**
- **If you want really good publicity lay siege to their building**
- **If you want really heart-warming publicity catapult burning balls of tar into the upper floors**

I'M TRYING TO UNDERSTAND THE YOUTH MARKET

Advertising Executives

What they say...	And what they mean...
All our evidence shows	You're not going to believe this
This is a major opportunity	We need your money
We'll certainly consider that	We won't do it
That's a good point, but...	I've heard some crap in my time...
We've been thinking	Because you obviously haven't
There's a lot of support for this concept	This is our only concept
May I make a suggestion?	Do this or you're neck deep in cack
That's a challenging brief	You haven't thought this through
Let me play devil's advocate	Let me stick a trident up your backside
We'll need to visit the factory	We know you have a factory in Florida
We won't need to visit the factory	We know you have a factory in Swindon
This is award winning work	You won't understand this
We've taken a radical approach	We gave this job to students
We'd like to challenge your brief	We haven't done the work yet
We've done a lot of brand analysis	The invoice is bigger than you expected
We've had a breakthrough with your product	You won't recognise anything you're about to see
Our creatives were very excited by this project	I did this because the creatives wouldn't touch it
This wouldn't work in print	We need to go on television
Radio wouldn't do this justice	We need to go on television
Posters are too static for this	We need to go on television
Our creative director worked on this one	If you don't buy it, you can tell him
We're going to do sketchbook presentation	We scribbled this lot down in the lift on the way up
We've stretched your brand's equities	We worked on the wrong brief
We've had three teams working on this	This presentation will be very confused
I can sense your excitement	Hello, is anybody home?
We'll go away and refine these concepts	We'll start from scratch
We must have a meeting one day	We might bump into each other

RESEARCH
❏ Ask a stupid question...

I f you're ever stopped in the street by a smart middle aged lady with a clipboard who asks you intimate questions, you are either participating in market research or being propositioned by an astonishingly inept streetwalker.

There are three sorts of market research; quantitative, where you ask how many people do things; qualitative, where you ask why people do things; and manipulative, where you just make things up. Take for example a disastrous West End show. Quantitative research would say that ninety-seven per cent of people hated it. Qualitative would tell you that people hated it because it was 'the theatrical equivalent of colonic irrigation'. Manipulative research would tell you that the show was 'Unmissable, fight to get a ticket!'

Hiring a research company is for corporate chickens. It's like asking a friend to ask someone else if they fancy you. If they're really your friend they're not going to come rushing back with 'She thinks you're repulsive and you make her sick'. So when you have a product like Bat Dung Moisturiser which people would think twice about putting on their compost let alone their face, don't be surprised when your highly paid research agency comes rushing back with, 'It's a winner, let's go with it'.

Not all research takes place on the street. Consumer labs are where you get a group of like-minded people in a cosy room with sofas and then you pay to sit behind a two way mirror and watch them perform. If these research groups lasted thirty seconds people would just say 'Yeah, that deodorant smells good, I'd put it in my armpit'. Instead they last three hours during which deodorant gradually becomes a metaphor for post-modern introspection and millennial angst. People say many things in research but one thing always remains unsaid and that is, 'Of course I wouldn't spend any of my money on that'.

KEY LEARNINGS
- **Middle-aged ladies with clipboards have the opposite effect of a truth drug**
- **Consumers change their mind shortly after you've spent millions launching a new product they said they loved**
- **Research has never been done on whether research works**

THE POST ROOM
❏ Dealing with primitive cultures

I f you ever look closely at a medieval painting you'll always find hideously deformed and badly dressed peasants lurking somewhere in the background. Their direct descendants can be found in the post rooms of major companies.

In the post room, brains that are already on a low energy setting have been reduced further in effectiveness by the licking of countless gummed envelopes. In fact the post room spend most of their day licking the glue that people under bridges sniff to escape from reality, which may go some way to explain why the lads down there have only a passing acquaintance with reality. In addition, there are many other toxic pollutants in the post room such as photocopy toner, magic markers and visiting despatch riders.

The post room is home to the company's pigeon holes, so called because they're generally full of unpleasant droppings. Sadly the days of pigeon holes are numbered, which is a shame because it will be difficult to leave someone's old squash shoes and athletic support on their e-mail. In the post room you will also find the franking machine which is an electronic social secretary that makes sure everyone's party invitations get out on time and at minimum cost.

The post room is a friendly place and the boys in there will always have the kettle on, generally because they'll be about to steam open your personal mail. Some post rooms still deliver mail to your desk and they will spend many happy hours practising throwing mail on to desks so that they can knock a cup of coffee over a computer keyboard at forty yards.

All the big courier companies guarantee to deliver your vital package anywhere in the universe overnight. Sadly that's not much help when the post room boy has left it under a pile of *Which Clutch?* Nevertheless, there are absolute deadlines that you have to stick to with the post room. At five o'clock sharp the mail goes, because the post room manager has to be on his way home at that time.

KEY LEARNINGS
- **The post room is the earthy hub of the modern corporation**
- **Life in all its infinite variety is found there**
- **Especially the microbiotic kind**

OFFICE NERDS

❏ The case for corporate quarantine

Some companies believe that public perception of their business will be substantially enhanced by getting their staff to wear brown viscose ties with their logo printed on the middle. Amazingly there are men who choose to wear these ties for social occasions because they look so snappy. These men are office nerds.

Office nerds have sandwiches that smell. They prepare them late at night and put in things like beetroot and creosote. Then they wrap them in cling film and stuff them into their trouser pocket. At lunch time they pull out a crushed mess, pick it open and release a foul smell, just when you are showing someone grotesquely important around the office.

Office nerds wear special shirts that cannot be tucked in at the back. Their suits are made from some of the nastier by-products of the chemical industry and their jackets are the sort that are refused by charity shops in case they drag the image of the shop down. This is all capped with hair styled by blowtorch and breath that would take the barnacles of a tug's hull. One word of warning. If you ever find yourself in intimate conversation with someone on the internet, however good-looking they say they are in real life, they will be a fully paid up office nerd.

The Byzantine workings of fate dictate that office nerds always hold a low paid, low charisma job which happens to be absolutely vital to the business. This usually involves ownership of a vital form that you can't have until you have been bored to the point of suicide with the nerd's hilarious sandpaper story. Corporations come and go, huge fortunes are made and lost, but nerds remain with rock-like permanence. The big mystery with office nerds is that at some stage a personnel manager must have said, 'yes, we've got to have this man in the company'.

KEY LEARNINGS
- Nerds wear vests tucked into the back of their pants
- Nerds tuck their shirt tails into the back of their pants
- Nerds tuck their suits into the back of their pants

Executive Committee of World Council of Office Nerds 1997–8

Rod Snot (Chairnerd)
Walter Suit
Barry Nobshine
Hector Nacho
Mike Merkin
Damien Slugpit
Norbert Norge
Payton Lee Obvious
Oliver Failure
Randolph Swipe
Denzel D. Oderant
Annuncio Llama
Gaston le Pong
Ralphy Pinkel
Jeremy Cupcake

OFFICE JUNIORS
❏ The bright side of child exploitation

I n this country we're very lucky that we don't have child labour because children are a nightmare to work with; they're creative, enthusiastic and like to do things straight away. Nevertheless most companies take on one or two young people as Office Juniors. These are carefully selected for being totally devoid of the above qualities and will be going through an intense period of depression the like of which the world has never seen and which no one can possibly understand. Such is the depth of their suffering that they are incapable of doing anything more complex than stapling two pieces of paper together.

Office juniors wear suits that fit at no more than three points on their body and they still do their tie up in a big fat knot to irritate the teachers.

They're also very good at wearing T shirts with obscenities printed on in huge letters and then suddenly appearing when you're showing important new clients around the building for the first time. The only way to communicate with office juniors is to secretly pop a pre-recorded tape into their Walkman that starts with a really depressing guitar riff (whatever a riff is) and then cuts into something like, 'Do what I asked you to do now, or I'll feed your other tape to the shredder.'

The worst kind of office junior is called Hugo who's having a year out before he goes to Cambridge. On his second day he'll be making helpful suggestions on delayering the organisation and reconfiguring internal value chains. It's always as well to listen to Hugo politely because his surname is very likely to have a spooky similarity to that of the Chairman. Of course that doesn't stop you dropping a tiny drop of Superglue onto his computer mouse and watching him drag two thousand quid's worth of equipment off the desk.

KEY LEARNINGS
- **Never patronise office juniors just because they're young and stupid**
- **We were all young once**
- **Except for Mrs Hatchet**

OFFICE CLEANERS
❏ All nature abhors a vacuum

Business re-engineering is what happens when expensive management consultants come into your company, completely rearrange all parts of your business and leave it totally unrecognisable. Cleaners do this on a nightly basis, except they don't charge a thousand pounds a day. It is estimated that cleaners accidentally take out five per cent of the gross national product in black bags at the end of each working day.

Some people say that the problem with cleaners is that they don't know the difference between a vital business document and what is genuine rubbish. This probably explains why so many cleaners naturally gravitate towards a career in PR.

Cleaners actually know a lot more about the health of companies than people who work in them; 'Oh yes, there were four drafts of the Operational Plan in the bin, because he couldn't make the figures work, poor love.' No one ever goes in the cleaner's cupboard because everyone assumes it's full of industrial strength Pledge. In fact, it's full of carefully reconstructed documents and a hot line for insider share dealing.

In high-tech offices you can transfer complex information around the world at the touch of a button. In the very same office it takes a machine that looks like a motorised bagpipe and sounds like Concorde to pick up a biscuit crumb. Ironically, cleaners themselves are incredibly efficient. They can dust, clean and polish three corporate headquarters and still be home in time for *EastEnders*.

Cleaners are no respecters of rank. The Board could be presenting the most crucial product in their history, but if they go on past seven they can expect the sound of the Hoover and a lady holding up their prize innovation asking 'Have you finished with this love?'

KEY LEARNINGS

- **An office can never be too clean, too busy or too far from Swindon**
- **When you sack all your cleaners it won't take long for the dust to settle**
- **If wasted time went into baskets, offices would look like wicker factories**

JOB SECURITY
❏ If you don't mind working late

Security guards are so called because the great majority of them are on social security and need somewhere to sleep at night. They all have names of one syllable at most, skin the colour of old sandpaper and body odour so virulent that it often sets off some of the more sensitive alarm systems.

There are two types of security guards. The first are criminals in fancy dress who come from companies called 'Tite Sekurity', work for a night or two to make a list of all the office valuables and then return later to remove them in an unmarked Transit van. The other sort is the permanent nightwatchman who is really one of the family – the unpopular member of the family you wouldn't want round at Christmas. The latter have more keys than a Wurlitzer organ and will unlock any door in the building for you as long as you simulate intense interest in five-a-side pigeon breeding or whatever their ludicrous daytime hobby is.

Nobody actually knows what security guards do in the wee small hours of the morning. If you come in first thing in the morning and you find your desk cleared and all your outstanding work done and piled neatly in your Out tray, it's a good bet that you haven't been visited by the fairy security guard. You've probably been sacked.

When all is said and done there is no one like a security guard in a time of crisis. If a fire rips through the building or there's an earthquake or a flash flood, the security guard will be the one person sure to die at their post – because generally they're absolutely fast asleep.

KEY LEARNINGS
- **Never ask to borrow ten pence from a security guard**
- **They never carry any cash on them**
- **Their pockets are on a time release security system with radio links to base**

Ten things that security guards do to pass the time

1 Scratch their nose	6 Check first floor
2 Pick their nose	7 Check second floor
3 Examine contents of nose	8 Check third floor
4 Roll contents of nose into small ball	9 Check Directors' floor
5 Check ground floor	10 Wipe fingers on MD's desk

~ CHAPTER 10 ~

LADIES, GENTLEMEN AND OTHERS

The definition of a gentleman in business is someone who
will always use a fish knife to stab you in the back if you're a Pisces.

Aidan Devlin ~ Twentieth-century Irish shaman and tax lawyer

GENTLEMEN
❏ If you can't hold it, let it go

It has taken man hundreds of thousands of years to evolve from a primitive savage to a high-tech master of the universe. To trace this evolution in reverse, simply step from any modern office into the Gentlemen's Toilet. Man can put a cruise missile through a bedroom window in Baghdad yet can't point Percy at the porcelain at point blank range.

There is a saying that you can tell a lot about the morale of a company by the state of its lavatories. If this is true then the whole of French industry must be in a state of deep and continuous depression. The lavatories in City institutions on the other hand are so spotless that you wonder if bankers ever have bowel movements. Knowing how difficult it is to get anything out of a banker, it's probably safe to assume they don't.

You can learn a lot about your colleagues in the washroom. For example you can get a little pip-squeak from accounts who doesn't touch tea or coffee all day, who has one Diet Ribena for lunch, and yet pees like a horse for well over five minutes. In general nothing halts the free flow of

NOW WIPE YOUR HANDS ON YOUR SUIT

urine faster than the Chief Executive pulling up in the stall next to you and saying 'How's your career coming along, Evans?' Especially if your name isn't Evans.

On your way out of the loo you can dry your hands in three ways. There is the roll on the wall that only lets you pull down one foot of towel for every ten thousand people who use it. Or there's the hot air blower which has the power of a ninety-year-old asthmatic and cuts out while your hands are still dripping wet. Finally there's what you do when there are no towels or blowers at all. This is where you can either wave your hands around briskly like you're trying to get rid of a very sticky sticky plaster and risk the Chief Executive strolling in again and thinking you're an absolute crackpot. Or you can go over to the pip-squeak from accounts who's still hosing down the ceramic and wipe your hands on the back of his suit.

KEY LEARNINGS
- **Forty-three per cent of executives do not wash their hands after downloading**
- **Never wash your hands before a crucial presentation unless you don't mind looking as if you've just missed the water jump in the steeplechase**
- **It's bad manners to pee longer than your boss if he's at an adjacent urinal**

LADIES
❏ The inside story

Ladies' lavatories are a lot like women's handbags – nothing special on the outside, but a whole world of fascination, mystery and excitement on the inside. Men have always wondered what goes on inside the Ladies, because if you happen to be walking past when the door is just closing, you can always hear women laughing and chatting and doing all sorts of marvellous fun things. You can imagine that inside there's a pool table, juke box, fridges full of exotic cocktails, beauty therapists applying seaweed to women's faces, wall-to-wall shag pile carpet, piped music, the aroma of lavender and primrose, large posters of Brad Pitt on the walls and blown up copies of *Cosmopolitan* articles entitled 'How to humiliate men in the bedroom and the boardroom'.

Ladies' lavatories must be something like this or what else would explain the queues. In the Seventies when there were mile-long queues to see the Tutankhamen exhibition, there was a lot of trouble when certain sections of the public realised they'd been waiting eight hours to get into the women's lavatories.

Of course there are other reasons why queues form and one is that women will do anything to avoid sitting down in the loo. They hang with both hands from the light fitting, or wedge themselves between the partition walls or use all available loo rolls to re-paper the cubicle from floor to ceiling. It doesn't help that there is only ever one cubicle in the ladies. That, of course, is because the rest of the space is taken up with exercise bikes, jacuzzis, Clinique counters, etc.

Once inside the Ladies, you then have to queue for the mirror. If a man spends more than three seconds in front of the mirror in the Gents, serious questions are raised about his sexuality, whereas women happily spend hours in front of the mirror doing anything from clipping their toe nails to a bit of do-it-yourself liposuction.

KEY LEARNINGS
- **Always make sure the hand dryer nozzle is pointing downward unless you want to look like Ken Dodd**
- **When travelling abroad always carry your own loo seat**
- **When travelling in France carry your own lavatory, cistern and connecting plumbing**

MEN'S OFFICE FASHION
❏ Getting office style buttoned down

One hundred years ago all working men from navvies to prime ministers wore a three-piece suit. They came in two colours; there was black for most people and for very creative types there was a deep charcoal grey. These days the choice of suit colours looks like the fabric book from Sofa City. But there is still one golden rule when it comes to suit colours – no one has ever, anywhere, made an impact or cut a dash in a brown suit.

All suits are not the same. Obviously there are the single-breasted, the double-breasted and the highly ostentatious triple-breasted. There are also subtle distinctions like the vents or slits up the back. There is the single vent that allows you to sit without creasing your jacket and then there is the double vent that looks like you have a cat flap in your bottom. Modern suits don't have any vents at all because they are designed by the same people who brought you the bin liner.

In some industries you don't have to wear a suit at all. In advertising what you wear in bed is generally more business-like than what you wear in the office. Here the impression you have to give is that you have been glued and thrown through a charity shop.

For the vast majority of men who wear the standard dark polyester suit, the only chance they have to express themselves is in their choice of tie. Which is why it comes as such a surprise that the message so many choose to express is 'I am a tasteless geek from the dark end of the void'.

If you're worried about the sort of suit you're wearing, count the buttons on the jacket. If there are more than three, then you are wearing some sort of weirdo creative combo and if you travel outside the M25 you run a real risk of having your underpants pulled over your head by unsympathetic builders.

KEY LEARNINGS
- You can't ask for a raise in a suit that cost less than £100
- You can't ask for a raise in a suit that cost more than your boss's entire wardrobe
- You can't ask for a raise in your birthday suit

Top ten fashion accessories for rural lawyers

1   Spats
2   Smock
3   Sword stick
4   Control girdle
5   Fob watch
6   Spurs and chaps
7   Swastika tie-pin
8   Monocle
9   Chilean Generalissimo epaulettes
10   Ammunition Bandoleer

WOMEN'S OFFICE FASHION
❑ Executive style comes out of the closet

Working women often fling open their wardrobe in the morning and complain that they have nothing to wear. Yet you never see women in the office wearing nothing. So something's not right there. When men fling open the wardrobe in the morning they see the same suit they have been wearing since school speech day, so agonising on what to wear is kept to an absolute minimum.

Power dressing was a phenomenon of the Eighties where women wore shoulder pads large enough to land a light aircraft on. Things have changed since then but there are still complex rules governing what you can and can't wear in the office. The one golden rule is that there is no such thing as power dressing in dungarees.

Skirt length is a good indicator of what sort of woman you're dealing with in the office. Slightly above the knee is your normal executive, well above the knee is your predatory Eighties' relic, well above the waist means adjustment is required after hasty visit to the Ladies. Skirts just above ankle denote elderly secretaries working in family engineering firm back office with tendency towards minor nervous ailments.

Women's jewellery has many meanings. Beware women with more rings than fingers, no good ever comes of them. Similarly beware women sporting a huge amount of jewellery all over their body. They are probably selling on commission and before you can say 'Tupperware' you'll be sitting in their front room getting the hard sell on some delightful mother of pearl brooch and tiara combo.

Women live in abject fear of walking into a meeting and being confronted with another woman wearing exactly the same outfit. Fortunately men don't feel the same way otherwise in every meeting there would be at least one man storming out saying 'Oh my God, he's got the M&S pin stripe. It's him or me.'

KEY LEARNINGS
- **Never say to a business woman, 'Oh it's that old dress again'.**
- **Especially if she's your boss**
- **And works in the fashion industry**

OFFICE ETHICS
❏ Where nice is a sort of biscuit

Being nice in the office is like being nice on the roads – everyone likes you but you don't actually get anywhere. Nice people bring homemade oat biscuits into work and leave out a plateful for everyone to help themselves. Dig into the soil surrounding any office pot plant and you will find these biscuits years later. Nice people also volunteer to make coffee. This is not necessarily a good thing because they cannot conceive of anybody actually liking strong coffee or tea and the only shade they make is what decorators would refer to as 'orchid white'.

Seriously nice people answer the phone when no one else does. They then proceed to take ownership of the piffling little concern of some irritating customer and make sure something happens. Naturally they will do this while neglecting their own vital work in the Health and Safety department and inevitably cause a horrific meltdown that kills and maims half the work force. Nice people are a menace.

It's very difficult to give nice people appraisals. For a start they give you a specially wrapped, takeaway parcel of homemade oat biscuits. You then have to tell them that despite their world famous niceness, their financial contribution to the growth of the company is zero. This is particularly difficult when they happen to be the Sales Director. Fortunately the chance of niceness and sales proficiency coexisting in one human being is fantastically remote.

Nice men have the added disadvantage of having the sexual attractiveness of a tea cosy. The only chance nice men have of going out with women is when they're recovering between absolute bastards. Nice men like to think that underneath that soft layer of niceness is an inner core of toughness. On closer examination this toughness usually turns out to be indigestion.

There are very few careers open to nice people. IT is a great place for nice people because people won't mind how nice you are, as long as you fix their bloody computer.

KEY LEARNINGS
- **Nice guys finish last**
- **With their faces trampled in the dirt**
- **And their women taken as booty**

Ten titles of business self-improvement books that have the opposite effect

1   Superhero in your Briefcase
2   Feel the Inner Woman
3   Light your Touchpaper and Retire
4   When Finance Directors Learn to Spit
5   Feel the Fear, Convulse and Throw Up
6   Awaken the Sycophant Within
7   Selling in Eight Easy Lessons, but for you only Six
8   How to make Fair Weather Friends and Lose Them when the Going Gets Tough
9   Making it Happen and Apologising for it Afterwards
10   You are You, Go with It

ORGANISED CRIME
❏ It's the only thing organised in business

You might be forgiven for thinking that the Serious Fraud Office is a polite euphemism for the headquarters of any of the privatised utilities. In fact it's a group of bitter sharp-nosed accountants and baffled old policeman who spend years unravelling complex financial scams only to have a jury acquit the perpetrators on the colour of their ties.

When they disband the Serious Fraud Office they should use the money to set up lots of little Petty Fraud Offices to come down hard on those people in every office that use the franking machine for their party invitations. Of course there are some people who would agonise about whether to take a biro home and wouldn't use the phone on their desk to phone their mother in hospital. Sadly, these saintly people tend to have short and very flat career paths.

Everyone uses office phones for social calls. In strict moral terms making social calls during office hours is theft from the company. But there's as much chance of business operating on strict moral terms as there is of Mother Teresa operating on strict business terms.

It's good to know that, while big businesses are busy stripping the third world of their resources and pensioners of their savings, their employees are equally busy stripping everything that moves from the company's offices. Most people occasionally take home a pen or a pad, but others merrily remove chairs, desks, pot plants and vital bits of industrial machinery. The most brazen example of this sort of behaviour is when a Chief Executive quietly takes home ten per cent of the entire worth of the company just by 'exercising his share options'. So next time Security catch you removing something from the office, tell them you're just exercising your share option.

KEY LEARNINGS
- If your boss forces you to take your work home, they can't object to you taking bits of the office as well
- Petty pilfering is anything that doesn't require a rented truck to take home
- Don't invite your boss round for dinner shortly after you've taken half the office furnishing home

---

CORPORATE FIRE-FIGHTING
❏ Living with total skin grafts

Fire drills are formal demonstrations to everyone in a company what it's like to be a smoker. You have to leave your desk at bizarre moments, make your way outside and then stand around in the cold for five minutes whingeing about things. Of course in a real fire the smokers would all be the first to die because after they'd been outside for five minutes they'd stub out their cigarettes and return to their desks.

Fire alarms by law have to be tested twice a year and if you were to take the time to read the actual wording of the statute, you would see that the law specifies that the bells must be rung when you have your trousers round your ankles in the executive washroom reading the diary section of *Hello!* Magazine.

Every office has a fire officer. This person has the responsibility for making sure that everyone from the office is accounted for. This is a lot trickier than it sounds because normal excuses won't do. It's no good telling the Fire Brigade that everyone's there apart from Mr Richard and Miss Philpott because they're 'in a meeting'. It's also a little known fact that more people are killed each year getting to assembly points than die in office fires. Look closely at the fire instructions in your office (they're behind the Spice Girls Calendar) and you'll notice that where you are asked to assemble is generally somewhere like 'Central reservation of M4' or 'Army firing range'.

Responsible offices make sure that at least three people are trained in the use of fire extinguishers. This training takes place during the office party when three national sales managers release high-pressure foam down the back of the office manager as a thank you for thirty years of continuous service.

KEY LEARNINGS
- **If you are used to continuous fire-fighting a real fire is a huge relief**
- **Every year nine Managing Directors in the UK spontaneously combust**
- **The one fireproof box in the office contains Darren's sandwiches**

Top ten Health and Safety violations of all times

Violator	Position	Accident
I. Ivanov	Cleaner	Chernobyl
S. Thomson	Graduate trainee	Three Mile Island
R. Sen	Habitual smoker	Bophal
S. Thomson	Stowaway	Exxon Valdez
L. Barry	Kwikbuck Cut Price Offal	B.S.E.
V. Thomson	Ex-royal ratcatcher	Black Death
S. Thomson	Fridge coolant technician	Global warming
E. Ubler	Purser and illicit smoker	Hindenberg disaster
H. Nachez	Keeper of Monkey House	Aids
S. Thomson	Fire Officer	Channel Tunnel

FALSIES
❏ There's no need to be alarmed

A feature of many offices these days is the false alarm. This is like a normal burglar alarm except for the fact that it isn't interested in going off when burglars are around. Instead it has a volatile Mediterranean temperament which means virtually anything will set it off. A moderately vigorous fart by a security guard will have bells ringing, lights flashing and sirens wailing. Which explains why all security guards have that sour, retentive look.

In smaller offices alarms are activated and de-activated by punching a four-number security code into a little keypad. Research, were someone dull enough to do it, would show that half of all these codes are 1234 or 1066 or the last four digits of the phone number of the building. These favourites are followed closely by 9999 which is chosen because no burglar would ever have enough time to go through all 9999 combinations.

In smaller offices the first person to arrive in the morning has to deactivate the alarm. Sadly the first person in is often the boss who can take you through every line of the annual report but has difficulty remembering the sequence 1234. This is when the alarm decides to put your boss in a great mood for the day by going off with nipple-piercing intensity for an hour or two until a secretary with a head for figures arrives.

Some alarms are linked to a security company who will phone the 'key holder' at any time during the day or night if the alarm goes off. The key holder then has to drive twenty miles in his Barney Rubble pyjamas to explain to four deeply unamused policemen why their alarm has to wake everyone in a three-mile radius just because a leaf has dropped off the receptionist's rubber plant.

KEY LEARNINGS
- **Superglue the leaves on the receptionist's rubber plant**
- **Ask not for whom the bell tolls if you're a key holder**
- **While working, professional burglars like to hum 'You can ring my bell'**

RECYCLING
❏ It's better second time around

Recycling has always been an essential part of business in that most people are selling the same old things at the same old price to the same old people. These things may look new because it's the job of the advertising industry to recycle fashionable art and apply it to the good old-fashioned toilet cleaner to make it seem the hippest, coolest, funkiest new thing you'd ever want to chuck down the lavatory.

Recycling in the office is catching on with special bins for recyclable paper. If these bins were for anything people in the office had written that was absolute rubbish, virtually all paper would be recycled. In fact a large part of the working day could be saved if printers from people's computers fed directly into these waste bins. It's pretty certain that if you had to pay a 5p deposit on every sheet of A4 paper you used, the paperless office would spring up overnight and the internal memo would be as rare as a hairy-chested Human Resources Director.

Naturally the one other thing in the office that you have to recycle is the one thing that you most want to throw away and never see again – the photocopier toner cartridge. (It can't in fact be recycled and it's all just a sales drive by the dry cleaning industry.)

Some firms are so environmentally conscious that they even recycle their people. They sack about half of them every year and then spend the rest of the year and thousands of pounds recruiting different people to do exactly the same job.

Of course no one is more serious about recycling than senior management and that is why they insist on having a new car every year and also returning all your work to you untouched, unread and unnoticed so you can do it all again.

KEY LEARNINGS
- **If it's going to be recycled why bother using it in the first place**
- **Never bio-degrade in a crowded lift**
- **Environmental Officers should be recycled whenever their beard reaches their astrological pendant**

SUMMER IN THE CITY
❑ Back of my neck getting hot and sweaty

E very few years all work in Britain comes to a grinding halt. It's because of something that makes train strikes seem a minor inconvenience. It's something called summer. There are only three air-conditioned offices in the whole of Britain and these are reserved for visiting Americans who can only work in temperatures between 64° and 68°. British workers regulate their temperature by becoming almost totally inert and fanning themselves with documents marked 'For immediate action'.

There is something that summer brings out in everyone and that is sweat. Middle managers wear shirts made out of the toxic by-products from heavy industry with labels that say 'Rich in Polyuranium. Poor in Cotton'. Wearing these shirts is the hygiene equivalent of wrapping yourself in cling film and not surprisingly middle managers only have to lift a pen for sweat stains the size of Luxembourg to spread across their shirts in a matter of seconds. If they then decide to stand in front of a fan in an open plan office, it has the same effect as a dust cart full of rotting fruit and veg backing up to an office window and belching.

Behaviour on roads deteriorates in the heat. People open their sun roofs, sit in traffic roasting their heads for a couple of hours and then wonder why they get snappy when someone forgets to indicate. If the temperature gets absolutely stifling in the office some of the more considerate bosses will take pity on their workers and let them go home before it gets dark.

In high summer secretaries rush out to buy fans. During the winter months these fans must find their way back to the shops because at exactly the same time the following year secretaries rush out and buy more fans.

Business clothing doesn't last long in the heat. First the jackets come off, then the ties, then someone wears shorts and finally some idiot goes and spoils it all by coming to work in a G-string. And let's face it, there's nothing worse than having your annual appraisal with your boss when he's sitting in his big leather chair wearing nothing but a thong.

KEY LEARNINGS
- **Wearing shorts in the office is an admission of no ambition**
- **When your armpit sweat stains meet your groin sweat stains it's time to change shirts**
- **When the heat is on check that the heating is not also on**

THE CHRISTMAS SPIRIT
❏ How to exploit it mercilessly

I n the office you know Christmas is on the way when you get a card from the company that supplies the glue for your carpet tiles, specially signed by Trevor, Carol and what looks like Ynathg, possibly their new Bosnian adhesive specialist. Christmas in the office is a marvellous magical time when everyone celebrates the arrival of the long heralded, much discussed and universally revered figure, the Christmas bonus. Sadly not all companies have a Christmas bonus and instead employees are allowed to go home fifteen minutes early on Christmas day.

Adults believe in the Christmas bonus with the same passionate enthusiasm as kids under three believe in Santa Claus and when they're finally told that the bonus doesn't really exist they react in the same utterly devastated way. Perhaps this is because by this stage they've already spent approximately double what they were expecting to get from their bonus. It's a bit different if you've got share options, which is like having Santa Claus parked in your drive all year round.

You can tell how good your bonus is by seeing how long you're prepared to stay with the company to get it. If you decide in early March that you can't possibly work for that evil dwarf a moment longer yet you're prepared to stick it out until the Christmas bonus, then in all probability it's a substantial one. The danger then is that you're so happy with your bonus and it's so cold outside, that you decide to stay on for another year, and before you know it you've been working at the same place, for the same evil dwarf, for forty years and you're the natural choice to play Father Christmas in the Personnel Department's Christmas grotto.

KEY LEARNINGS
- **Never buy your boss a Christmas present**
- **If it's cheap and nasty they won't like it**
- **If it's expensive and tasteful you won't get a pay rise**

Ten Great British companies that are no longer with us

1   British Pith (Helmet) Co.
2   Llandudno Fried Chicken
3   The Imperial Ivory, Whale Oil, Tiger Skin,
     Seal Pelt Importers Ltd
4   21st Century Carbon Paper
5   Future Vision Industrial Clairvoyancy
6   British International Spam
7   Middle Eastern Beer, Wine and Spirits Exports Ltd.
8   Colonial Irrigation Ltd
9   Spats r Us
10   British Leyland

Q&A5 DO YOU REALLY ENJOY YOUR JOB
Try this Standard Employee Attitude Survey

1. How satisfied are you with your current employment?

A   Have rarely been happier
B   Continual rippling orgasm
C   Rich inner contentment and peace
D   Other high levels of ecstasy

2. When you get up on a Monday morning do you . . .

A   Sing 'What a wonderful world' in the shower
B   Rejoice in your many blessings and sing the praises of your
     employer
C   Kiss a photo of your boss and stare at a framed copy of
     your wages slip
D   All of the above combined with a feeling of utter
     unspeakable joy

3. What is your ideal salary bracket?

A   Minimum wage
B   £4–6K
C   £5–7K
D   Charitable status

4. On a scale of 1–10, how satisfied are you with your current remuneration?

10

❑   Other. [Please tick box and clear your desk.]

5. If you were to receive your P45 would you . . .

A   Go quietly

B   Download confidential database and sell to competition

C   Empty Uzi fully automatic machine pistol into board meeting

6. If you answered A to previous question please collect P45.

7. How well do you think you have you done your job in the last twelve months?

A   What job is that?

B   Not well enough to deserve any more money

C   Monkeys could do my job

D   I've done all I can, please let me go

8. Is your boss . . .

A   Good looking

B   A superb leader

C   Hung like a brontosaurus

D   Standing right behind you

9. For our records how much stationery have you pilfered in the last twelve months?

A None at all and I pray for those who have

B Only essential requirements of friends, family and neighbours

C Equivalent to entire contents of WH Smith

D Enough to clear 115 hectares of Amazonian rainforest

10. Be honest for a moment and tell us if we are all:

A utter morons

B complete twats

C total wankers

D absolute tossers

[If you answered this question go to Question 6]

Thank you for your time and honesty and good luck in your next job.

INDEX